DATE DUE			
Dec 11 '80			
Apr 27 '83			

MAO TSE-TUNG AND GANDHI

MAO TSE-TUNG
AND
GANDHI

Perspectives on Social Transformation

JAYANTANUJA BANDYOPADHYAYA

Professor and Head of the Department of
International Relations
Jadavpur University

Sole distributors in the USA & Canada
PARAGON BOOK GALLERY, LTD.
14 EAST 38th STREET
NEW YORK, N.Y. 10016

ALLIED PUBLISHERS
BOMBAY CALCUTTA NEW DELHI
MADRAS BANGALORE

First Published 1973

ALLIED PUBLISHERS PRIVATE LIMITED

15 Graham Road, Ballard Estate, Bombay 1
5th Main Road, Gandhinagar, Bangalore 9
17 Chittaranjan Avenue, Calcutta 13
13/14 Asaf Ali Road, New Delhi 1
38-C Mount Road, Madras 6

PRINTED IN INDIA

BY P. K. GHOSH AT EASTEND PRINTERS, 3 DR SURESH SARKAR
ROAD, CALCUTTA 14 AND PUBLISHED BY R. N. SACHDEV FOR ALLIED
PUBLISHERS PRIVATE LTD, 17 CHITTARANJAN AVENUE, CALCUTTA 13

PREFACE

THIS BOOK MARKS the end of one phase of an essentially personal quest, inspired by a very old and intense interest in the problems of ideology and politics, almost to the point of an obsession. The ideological and political ferment in India in the first half of this century seemed to be a natural starting-point for this quest, and I chose the conflict between nationalism and communism in India during this period as the theme of my first major work. The central conclusion of this study was that the resilience and relative success of nationalism in India were largely due to the broad ideological content and organizational base imparted to it mainly by Mahatma Gandhi. And yet the impact of Gandhi on independent India did not seem to be great. What, then, are the points of strength and weakness of the theory and practice of Gandhism which proved efficacious in one historical context and less effective in another? This question led to my second major work, on the social and political thought of Gandhi. Meanwhile the relatively weak legacy of Gandhi in India seemed to be overwhelmed by the new impact of Maoism which drew large numbers of educated young people into its fold in many parts of India, especially in my own state of West Bengal. Elsewhere in Asia, too, the influence of Maoism was great and growing, while that of Gandhi was negligible and declining. Was China's way, then, also the way of India and other Afro-Asian states? But a serious investigation of this problem was delayed by the relative scarcity of source materials on Mao and China in this country. I utilized the time in producing a work on what really is, in spite of my past diplomatic career and present professional commitments, only my second love, namely, Indian foreign policy and its making. Problems of ideology and political development, in so far as they have a bearing on foreign policy, were briefly discussed in this work also, but the main inquiry had to be postponed. Two years of research and teaching at the

Columbia University, New York, and the American University, Washington D.C., enabled me to pursue the inquiry seriously and to articulate my own ideas on the subject. The result is the present work, which has been an exercise in self-education and is a tentative answer to a personal intellectual and emotional need. I fervently hope it answers similar needs of many others in this country and elsewhere.

I take this opportunity to express my sincere thanks to Professor Z. Brzezinski of Columbia University, who made my visit to Columbia possible, treated me with all the cordiality of a friend and stimulated me intellectually whenever we discussed anything. I am also thankful to my students at the American University, especially my graduate and Ph. D. students, from whom I learnt much, directly or indirectly, that has been useful to me in writing this book.

J. BANDYOPADHYAYA

Jadavpur University
Calcutta 32
13 March 1973

CONTENTS

CHAPTER ONE

HISTORICAL BACKGROUND

NOWHERE HAS THE multi-dimensional process of political, economic and socio-cultural transformation[1] unfolded itself on so vast a scale and in so fascinating a manner as in China and India, and no other leaders and thinkers have influenced the course of this unfolding Asian drama by their ideas and actions more than Mao Tse-tung and Gandhi. The alternative models of social transformation progressively developed by the two great Asian leaders represent certain ideological perspectives and tools of social engineering peculiarly related to the given historical and socio-political situations in China and India, and it is on the question of the efficacy or otherwise of these two alternative models in the context of the developing societies that the ideological battle in the third world is being fought. Elsewhere in the world, too, the influence of the ideas of these two Asian leaders on the minds of men, especially the younger generation, seems to be growing. It is my purpose in this book to analyse and critically examine the Maoist and Gandhian approaches to social transformation in their specific Asian context, and to derive lessons, as far as possible, for the future course of development elsewhere. Towards the end of the study I shall also endeavour to discuss briefly the relevance of the ideas of Mao and Gandhi to some of the problems of the industrial societies.

For a variety of reasons it is difficult to estimate accurately the impact of a leader or an ideology on the transformation of a society. In the first place, it is virtually impossible to find out what would have happened in the absence of a particular leader or ideology in a given situation. Conceivably, this century would have witnessed the rapid transformation of Asia even if neither Mao nor Gandhi was ever born, although their leadership and ideological approaches undoubtedly imparted specific contents to the process of change in

China and India. Secondly, it is difficult to isolate personalities and ideologies from other factors in the transformation process. Thirdly, an important distinction has to be made between the short-run and long-run impacts of leaders and ideologies on social change, since what may seem to be rapid progress in the short run often leads to relative instability and even partial disintegration in the long run, while apparently slow development in the short run may be the foundation for steady and more rapid progress in the long run.

An additional difficulty in comparing the roles played by Mao and Gandhi in the transformation of China and India respectively is caused by the generation gap between the two leaders. Gandhi, born in 1869, was twenty-four years older than Mao. Yet both he and Mao started participating actively in the national politics of their respective countries at about the same time, around the year 1920. Gandhi died five months after India's independence, without exercising any governmental power, whereas Mao has had the opportunity, for over two decades after coming to power, to guide the reconstruction of China according to his own ideological convictions, through the virtually unlimited use of state power. Moreover, sufficient time has elapsed since the death of Gandhi for a reasonably objective assessment of his influence on the process of change in India since independence, while the fate of Mao's thought in China after his death remains to be seen.

For all these reasons, a meaningful comparison between Mao and Gandhi from the point of view of the social transformation of China and India respectively can be made, not in terms of the general political, economic and socio-cultural development of the two countries since the twenties of this century, but in terms of the institutional and organizational innovations which can be attributed directly or indirectly to the two leaders. And this is the kind of comparison which has been attempted in this study.

The fundamental strategic problems faced by Mao and Gandhi in China and India in the early part of this century were formally similar in some important respects. Although China had not been under direct foreign rule like India, Western imperialism had indirectly imposed itself on that country in the nineteenth century through a form of gunboat diplomacy against a decaying Manchu regime; in fact one of the important causes of the fall of the Manchu dynasty was its inability to resist the increasing political and economic concessions wrested by the big powers from the proud inhabitants of the Middle Kingdom. Besides, much of Mao's political career in opposition was taken up by the resistance against Japanese imperialism in the 'thirties and 'forties. His fight against the Kuomintang in the last phase of the civil war had also powerful anti-Western overtones, since the former received large-scale military and economic assistance from the USA. Hence, although Mao's objective was the seizure of power from a national government, historical Western imperialism in China, Japanese imperialism and Western backing for the Chinese Nationalist Government gave his struggle the character of a fight by a predominantly agrarian and militarily weak population against industrially and militarily powerful adversaries—essentially the same kind of struggle that Gandhi had to organize in India against British rule.

But Mao regarded the struggle against the Japanese and the Kuomintang as only a necessary precondition to the development of China along Marxist-Leninist lines, just as Gandhi regarded the ending of British rule as a mere prelude to the transformation of India according to his own ideological convictions. To both the leaders, the principal and long-term task was the general reconstruction of their societies. And in this respect also, the strategic problem faced by them was essentially the same. Approximately 80 per cent of the population in both the countries lived in the agricultural sector, which was characterized by semi-feudal and exploitative relations of production, fragmentation and subdivision of holdings, considerable tenancy, landlessness and disguised unemployment, and abysmal poverty. It was this predominantly agrarian population which had to be not only the main force in the political (as well as military in the case of China) struggle, but also the principal factor in the process of change. All political strategies and tactics, all plans and programmes of economic development, all social and cultural change including the style and content of education, and the general ideological framework had to be geared to the mobilization, galvanization and uplift of this amorphous, oppressed and famished peasant mass. Much of the thinking of Mao and Gandhi with regard to social transformation, as well as their practical experiments, can be understood only in the context of this fundamental, palpable and hard reality.

But in view of the age-old mass illiteracy of the peasantry as well as the negligible size and illiteracy of the industrial working class in both the countries, the leadership of the peasant masses had to come from the middle class—a class which Marx and Engels had regarded as at best a fickle and unreliable ally of the peasants and workers, although Lenin had assigned a more positive role to it. As is well known, classical and imperial China had a powerful intellectual tradition, and the scholar occupied the highest position in a society regulated by Confucian mores. It was from the intelligentsia that China's administrators were traditionally recruited through a system of competitive examinations, which led to the development of the unique Chinese class of scholar-bureaucrats. It was a group of intellectuals led by K'ang Yu-wei and Liang Ch'i-ch'ao that demanded drastic political and economic reforms towards the end of the nineteenth century, an abortive attempt to introduce some of which on the part of the child emperor was foiled by Empress Dowager. Sun Yat-sen himself was more of an intellectual than a politician, and the moving spirit behind the revolution led by him was the Chinese intelligentsia. But Sun was not able to provide a coherent and practical ideology, or to raise an organized army, or to unify the country politically and administratively. The failure of the revolution led by him finally disillusioned large sections of the intelligentsia, and many intellectuals and reformers started demanding a complete break with the past economically, politically and even socially. The First World War accelerated the process. The Chinese intelligentsia was in a rebellious, bewildered, inarticulate, fumbling and groping mood when it felt the impact of the Russian Revolution, and when the May Fourth Movement, initially caused by the unfair treatment meted out to China at Versailles, galvanized the intellectuals and students into concerted political action, and perhaps most important of all, drew Mao Tse-tung into the maelstrom of Chinese politics. It is this middle class intelligentsia which has provided the leadership to the Chinese Communist movement under the overall guidance of Mao Tse-tung. In India, too, it was the Western-educated intelligentsia, inspired by the rediscovery of the cultural, intellectual and even political splendour of ancient India on the one hand, and British and French political thought, the history of the American War of Independence and the French Revolution on the other, that not only initiated a cultural renaissance but also generated a political nationalism in the second half of the nineteenth century, symbolized by the founding of the Indian National Congress in 1885. British imperialism and racialism in India, Lord Curzon's attempt to partition Bengal in 1905, the inadequacy of the Reform Acts of 1909 and 1919, the infamous Rowlatt Bills of 1918 which sought to nullify whatever fundamental liberties were then enjoyed by the Indian people, and the British atrocities in the Punjab in 1919 were the major domestic factors which fuelled the indignation of this middle class intelligentsia, while its imagination received nourishment from such external factors as Japan's victory over Russia in 1905, the Russian revolution of the same year, the Chinese revolution led by Sun Yat-sen in 1911, the First World War, De Valera's exploits in Ireland and the Russian Revolution of 1917. It was a large section of this middle class intelligentsia which constituted Gandhi's immediate following and provided the leadership, under the overall supervision of Gandhi, to the national movement in India. The historical function of both Mao and Gandhi was to organize this intelligentsia politically and yoke it firmly to the service of the real people of their respective countries, namely, the peasantry.

The political movements led by Mao and Gandhi had also a common psychological basis in nationalism. In the nineteenth century Chinese nationalism was directed partly against Manchu imperialism and partly against Western imperialism which the Manchu rulers had in turn been unable to resist. If the Taiping Rebellion was primarily anti-Manchu in its aim, the Boxer Rebellion was primarily anti-Western. The revolution of 1911, though resulting in the overthrow of the Manchus, had strong anti-Western overtones. It was on this pre-existing base of Chinese nationalism that Mao Tse-tung tried to build the habitation of the internationalist ideology of Marxism-Leninism during the long struggle of the Chinese Communist Party for power. Anti-Western feeling in general and anti-American feeling in particular has always been strong in Mao and his followers since the Treaty of Versailles when China felt let down by the USA, but from the early 'twenties to the end of the Second World War Chinese nationalism was primarily preoccupied with Japanese imperialism. The latter, Mao argued during this period, had driven China's historical conflict with Western imperialism into the background. In fact he became a strong advocate of a policy of seeking aid from the Western powers during the War of Resistance against Japan and even praised them for aiding and assisting China in the anti-Japanese struggle. It was not until the end of the Second World War and the beginning of the last stage of the civil war in 1946 that Mao started regarding the USA as the principal imperialist enemy. Since then the tempo of Chinese nationalism has been maintained by anti-Western-ism in general and anti-Americanism in particular, and since 1956 also by anti-Sovietism. Mao has constantly glorified this Chinese nationalism, thus going against the orthodox Marxian view of nation-alism (as Stalin did in Russia), and Sinified Marxism-Leninism in a manner which we shall analyse subsequently. Gandhi, too, in spite of his belief in the "voluntary interdependence" rather than unfettered independence of nations and his idealization of the human race as a global family, operated essentially within the broad framework of the Indian national movement which had developed to a consider-able extent before his return from South Africa and spectacular entry into the Indian political scene. In fact he was responsible, more than anyone else, for broadening the base of the national movement and increasing its organizational strength. Although he endeavoured, with considerable success, to inform the entire nationalist movement with ethical and cultural values, and to keep in check the chauvinistic and aggressive tendencies which are generally characteristic of all nationalisms, none of his political, economic or socio-cultural pro-grammes, nor the major mass movements led by him, can be visual-ized except in the broad psycho-political context of the Indian national movement. In the given historical context, both Mao and Gandhi have been compelled to operate on the broad platform of nationalism in spite of their internationalist ideological convictions.[2]

One corollary of this historical compulsion was the need felt by both Mao and Gandhi for uniting the populations of their countries on as big a common and undivided front as possible. Although Mao's theoretical modus operandi was the class struggle which essentially meant, in the given situation, the seizure of power from the Kuomin-tang, in practice the most formative part of his political career and ideological thinking was taken up by efforts to forge a working al-liance between the Communist Party and the Kuomintang. In the 'twenties this policy was partly dictated by the relative weakness of the Communist Party but largely by the Soviet Government and the Comintern which were at this time following the Leninist policy of utilizing the national movements in the East for weakening the Western powers and their political systems; and in the 'thirties (after a brief interregnum of open hostility against the Kuomintang) and first half of the 'forties by the Japanese invasion. Even in the "liberated areas" of the north, Mao did not carry the class struggle beyond preliminary land reforms, and accepted the cooperation of whatever bourgeois elements were in existence. Since, according to Mao's own analysis of class relations in China, the Kuomintang represented the exploiting classes while the Communist Party represented the peasants and workers, the united front with the Kuomintang practically throughout the life of the Chinese Communist Party in opposition represented an unavoidable compromise dictated by the given historical situation, especially by the historically given character of Chinese nationalism. Even after the seizure of power by the Chinese Communist Party Mao felt the need for maintaining a broad common front of the masses for the purpose of the socio-economic reconstruction of China, and was rather cautious, as we shall see, in advocating open struggles among classes strictly in accordance with Marxist theory. Gandhi was opposed, like Mao and other Marxists, to the exploitation of the peasants and workers by the landlords and capitalists, and advocated active nonviolent resistance to the latter on the part of the former, but in the given historical situation had to concentrate his energies on building the broadest possible mass front against British imperialism. He could not, therefore, concern himself primarily with the problem of resolving class contradictions in British India even through the nonviolent method, since that would have divided the national movement and dissipated its energies internally, thus weakening its resistance against British rule. He has been criticized by Marxists in India and abroad for this policy of "class collaboration," but it is difficult to see what other policy he could have followed in the given historical situation, just as it is difficult to see how Mao could have avoided a similar policy of "class collaboration" in the given historical situation in China. The major difference between Mao and Gandhi in this respect seems to be that while Mao has lived to attempt the implementation of his radical programmes in a different historical situation, Gandhi did not.

But these basic similarities in the historico-strategic situations faced by Mao and Gandhi were matched by equally important differences in the historical situations in which they found themselves. Perhaps the most important of these differences was the contemporary political conditions in China and India. When Mao Tse-tung appeared on the Chinese political scene, China was characterized by highly unstable political conditions and a good deal of socio-political unrest. Western imperialism, though largely indirect, had eaten into the vitals of Chinese political life. The authority of the central government was limited, and the country was virtually ruled by numerous local warlords, fighting against one another and against the central government. Even the political position of the intelligentsia had been undermined by the abolition of the system of competitive examinations for recruitment to the bureaucracy early in this century, leading simultaneously to a virtual breakdown of administration and the alienation of the intelligentsia from the government. Extreme despotism characterized the rule of the warlords and any form of protest against their unbridled tyranny was usually crushed by sheer brute force. In the midst of these chaotic political conditions a powerful nationalism was growing since the end of the nineteenth century, and some abortive attempts at introducing drastic reforms were made in the last days of Empress Dowager's reign. But in the absence of an intellectual and cultural renaissance in China in the nineteenth century (which took place in India and Japan and gave an ideological content to the national movements in these countries), Chinese nationalism remained characterized by a certain ideological vacuum which manifested itself forcefully in the blind and aimless fury of the Boxer Rebellion. Even Sun Yat-sen's revolution and his syncretic ideology of the Three Principles failed to fill this vacuum. His programme for the rapid economic development of China primarily with massive foreign aid was consistent neither with the realities of international politics nor perhaps with the prevailing mood of the Chinese intelligentsia. The failure of the Kuomintang either to unify the country under a strong central government or to implement the Three Principles, and its corrupt and inefficient administration increasingly alienated it from the peasantry and the intelligentsia. The situation demanded a strong, disciplined and incorruptible national political party with a definite ideology and programme, as Bertrand Russell pointed out in 1922.[3] In the given situation the Communist Party alone was able to answer this crying political need. No other ideology except Communism was able, in the given conditions, to provide the avant-garde political philosophy which would have been in tune with the radical spirit of Chinese nationalism as manifested in the May Fourth Movement, as Harold Isaacs has rightly observed.[4] Moreover, the failure of the revolution of 1911 and the situation which developed during the 'twenties and 'thirties indicated that no other party except the Communist Party had the ideological and organizational strength necessary to implement even the relatively moderate reform programme of Sun Yat-sen, especially the programme of land reform. Chinese nationalism was radical and revolutionary in spirit, but ideologically and organizationally in a state of vacuum. The Chinese Communist Party led by Mao in a sense naturally filled this void. The fortuitous and external circumstance of the prolonged Japanese invasion helped the party to identify itself further with Chinese nationalism (and thus to consolidate its political and military position) by laying bare the organizational and military bankruptcy of the Kuomintang on the one hand, and by demonstrating its own fighting zeal and organizational power on the other.

India, on the other hand, had been directly under British rule for a hundred and seventy-five years when Gandhi appeared on the political scene. The country had been politically and administratively unified and law and order established under a strong central government which did not permit the existence of any local military satraps or other organized armed groups which could seriously challenge the military power of the regime. The population as a whole had in fact been debarred from owning, possessing or carrying any kind of firearms. British imperialism in India, moreover, was not only more liberal than other imperialisms elsewhere, it was considerably more tolerant than the warlords under whom most of the Chinese people lived. In spite of many instances of brutality, it tolerated political opposition to a considerable extent, and had in fact actively encouraged the founding of the Indian National Congress, probably with a view to preventing the growing national movement from channelizing itself into insurrectionary activities. Even after the Congress had started fighting for India's independence and organized mass movements under Gandhi's leadership which seriously challenged British power in India, the entire national movement was on the whole treated with a measure of leniency by the British Government which was unthinkable under the Chinese warlords. Another evidence of the relatively liberal character of British rule in India was the general constitutional evolution towards national self-government, especially from 1909 to 1935. It is no small tribute to British imperialism in India that out of the 395 Articles of the Constitution of free India, 250 have been absorbed from the Government of India Act, 1935 under which the Congress exercised considerable power in India, especially in the provinces, long before independence. The constitutional concessions reluctantly but progressively granted by the British were of course the result of the national movement itself; but the fact remains that these involved educated Indians in the political and governmental process and induced them to become professional administrators and politicians rather than professional revolutionaries. Finally, the cultural renaissance of the second half of the nineteenth century, itself partly the result of political stability and Western education, had imparted an ideological content to the national movement which had strong roots in the national cultural tradition, and was absorbed politically by the Indian National Congress. By 1920 the Indian national movement had developed a set of powerful indigenous ideals which gave it a distinctive ideological character and frustrated the efforts of the Soviet Government and the Comintern to convert it into a Communist movement, as I have tried to show elsewhere.[5] What the national movement lacked before Gandhi assumed its leadership was a truly mass character and, therefore, a true Indian identity. Both the Moderates and the Extremists, who represented the two main wings of the Congress, had been unable either to achieve any significant results or to involve the masses of India in organized political action. Neither petitioning the British Government nor assassinating Englishmen through individual terrorism had succeeded in any way. It remained for Gandhi to impart a mass character and a national identity to the freedom movement and to lead it into extraconstitutional, direct, nonviolent and militant struggle.

The economic conditions in the two countries, in spite of their common agricultural character, were also considerably different. Land yields as well as total and per capita agricultural production in China were much higher than those of India, largely due to depleted soil fertility in India and much larger application of fertilizers in China.[6] This meant that the Chinese peasants, though poor, were considerably better off than their Indian counterpart—one of the many evidences of the fact that revolutions are not caused by economic distress alone. The poverty of the Indian peasants was further aggravated by the destruction of India's traditional cottage industries and handicrafts by British industrial competition and the colonial economic policy of the British Government. On the other hand, since the British Government was able to establish an effective administration and to keep the feudal hierarchy under complete control, feudalism in India was not nearly as oppressive as in China, where the political licence enjoyed by the feudal gentry often enabled them to put an economic squeeze on the peasantry which occasionally compelled the lowest strata of the peasants and landless labourers to leave their lands and become roving bandits. Moreover, whereas the system of transport and communication in China was extremely backward, which partly explained the inability of the central government to extend its authority over the whole country and the ability of insurrectionary movements to sustain themselves in isolated areas, the British in India had built an elaborate network of roads, railways, post and telegraph which facilitated the economic, political and administrative integration of the whole country. Finally, while the long Sino-Japanese war threw the Chinese economic system completely out of gear, which now became predominantly characterized by falling production and runaway inflation, thus further aggravating economic distress and promoting political extremism, in India the economic system, though on the whole nearly stagnant, maintained a relative stability and even registered some gains during the Second World War.

Another major difference lay in the socio-political character of the peasantry in the two countries. Traditionally the Chinese peasantry was infinitely more politicized and revolutionary than the Indian. From ancient times there had been hundreds of peasant insurrections in China, and practically every Chinese empire had been brought down partly by armed peasant uprisings—a fact explained by Barrington Moore in terms of the economic and social alienation of a large section of the peasantry and the weak link between the peasantry as a whole and the government.[7] In this century also the peasantry provided the most fertile source of the mercenary armies of the numerous Chinese warlords. Mao in fact made a deep study of the peasant revolts in Chinese history, regarded them as unparalleled in world history in their intensity, frequency and dimensions, and declared them to be the prime mover of Chinese history.[8] There is no comparable history of peasant revolts in India,[9] where the peasantry as a whole seems to have remained completely depoliticized from the ancient times, refusing to be concerned with changes of rulers or governments—a fact which may perhaps be best explained by the *varnashrama dharma* or caste duty which made politics and warfare the responsibility of the Kshatriyas rather than of the Shudras that the peasants were. Secondly, the Chinese peasantry, and for that matter the entire Chinese population, had a this-worldly, matter-of-fact and largely areligious outlook from ancient times. In spite of the spread of Buddhism in China, the daily lives of the Chinese peasantry remained anchored to Confucian mores which were atheistic in origin and emphasized family duties and correct social relationships. Social life as a whole in China had a broadly secular basis. In India, on the other hand, the peasant masses, like the people as a whole, were steeped in religion, had a somewhat fatalistic otherworldliness; and under the influence of Buddhism, Jainism and the devotional branch of Hinduism commonly called Vaishnavism, the bulk of the people had espoused nonviolence to the extent that a large section of the population had become vegetarian on religious grounds quite early in Indian history.[10] The Western education of the nineteenth and twentieth centuries failed to produce even a ripple in the basically religious ethos of the vast Indian masses. In formulating their ideological approaches, politico-economic programmes and methods of action, both Mao and Gandhi had to take serious note of these special characteristics of the peasantry—the bedrock of the social structure—in their respective countries.

And this leads us to the broad differences between the socio-cultural systems of the two countries. In spite of the privileged position of the warlords, feudal gentry and scholar-bureaucrats (there was considerable overlapping between the last two), China had a much more homogeneous and integrated society than the Indian. Occupations and social position were not hereditary in China, and the vast majority of the Chinese people represented a solid and socially mobile mass of humanity with a common language and culture. Religious minorities were too small and unimportant to cause any major social division. In India, on the other hand, the hereditary caste system, which has been identified by such otherwise mutually antagonistic scholars as Hegel, Marx and Max Weber as the main cause of India's socio-economic stagnation and political decay,[11] has traditionally stratified and immobilized Indian society into a multitude of micro-organismic social units maintaining an unequal and fundamentally hostile coexistence. Since ancient times the Brahmanas (the priestly class), Kshatriyas (rulers and soldiers) and Vaishyas (the merchant class), together constituting a very small minority of the population, have dominated, oppressed and exploited the Shudras (peasants and artisans) and the Asprishyas (untouchables engaged in "dirty work") who constitute the overwhelming majority of the people. Buddhism had to some extent emancipated and given a measure of human dignity to these vast masses of the underdog, but when Hinduism succeeded in destroying Buddhism in the early middle ages, it rehabilitated itself on the basis of a revitalized caste system. Since then the four original *varnas* or orders have multiplied into thousands of castes, subcastes and sub-subcastes, and neither Islam nor Christianity, neither the Bhakti movement of the middle ages nor the reform movements of the nineteenth century have been able to undermine the foundations of the caste system to any significant extent. And these myriad social divisions have been aggravated by great differences in religion (especially since the late middle ages), language and many other aspects of culture. The task of socio-political mobilization faced by Gandhi in India, therefore, was much more difficult than that of Mao in China.

Finally, there is the important question of the traditional politico-economic organization of civil society and its relationship with the state in India and China. In China the villages were traditionally organized on the basis of mutual aid and cooperation by family units and sometimes by clan groups, and had a far more egalitarian character than the Indian village *panchayets* which were usually run by the dominant castes with very little voluntary intercaste cooperation. The Indian villages, however, were far more self-managed and autonomous than their Chinese counterparts. Although there is some controversy regarding Karl Wittfogel's thesis that the Chinese governments traditionally exercised "oriental despotism" through their control over the hydraulic or irrigation system, it is generally agreed that the Chinese state always exercised a good deal of economic and political control over the villages, that all strong emperors tried to extend and consolidate this control, and that at least once in ancient Chinese history the state had nationalized land and distributed it among semi-militarized peasants on the basis of need and use.[12] In India, however, the village *panchayets*, the disappearance of which Marx regarded as a necessary precondition to the industrialization of India,[13] remained fully autonomous and self-managed through the centuries, indifferent to and even disdainful of the vast and continuous political upheavals on the surface of Indian social life. It was a tradition which even the British Government did not or could not seriously interfere with. In other words, while Indian social organization was more inequitous than the Chinese, it was definitely more autonomous and free from state control than the latter. Both Mao and Gandhi had to utilize and partially transform the two traditional systems for the reconstruction of their respective societies.

But the ideas and actions of the heroes of history are merely conditioned and not uniquely determined by given historical circumstances. There is always a strong subjective element in the way the socio-political milieu influences their personality in the formative period, which in turn conditions their reading and interpretation of the historical conditions in which they find themselves as mature individuals and the direction and manner in which they endeavour to steer the course of history. Thus although Mao's illiterate mother, to whom he was devoted, was a devout Buddhist, and he himself remained one until his adolescence, and although he learnt Confucian classics by heart in a primary school until the age of thirteen, neither Buddhism nor Confucianism had any formative influence on his mind. He was much more deeply influenced by his violent quarrels with his utilitarian and semi-literate father who opposed his education beyond the elementary level; by the exploits of the warrior-statesmen as narrated in such Chinese classics as *Romance of the Three Kingdoms*; and by the classical Chinese novel, *Water Margin*— the great traditional novel of Chinese peasant revolt against a corrupt government and bureaucracy, in which the rebels violently struck at the rich in order to help the poor. The international event which impressed him most in 1910 at the age of 17 was Japan's military success against Russia in 1905. About the same time he read considerable Western philosophy, politics and literature, including Marxism, but what impressed him most was a book called *Great Heroes of the World* which contained the biographies of Peter the Great, Catherine the Great, George Washington, the Duke of Wellington, Napoleon, Gladstone, Rousseau and Lincoln, and concluded that China needed great heroes like some of these in order to avoid the fate of India, Amman and Korea. He was also profoundly influenced by the Chinese military classic, Sun Tzu's *On the Art of War*, from which in fact he learnt many of his military strategies and tactics and borrowed heavily in his military writings. He made a deep study of the Taiping Rebellion, whose ideals and objectives were very similar to those of Marxism, but did not like its metaphysical overtones.[14] According to Stuart Schram, "from Japan to America, and from the modern West to ancient China, the figures which struck Mao's imagination and fired his enthusiasm were at once warriors and nationbuilders,"[15] and on the eve of the May Fourth Movement, when he was not yet a convinced Marxist, his "two most deeply etched traits appear to have been an emphasis on military strength and heroism and a vigorous nationalism."[16] It was this Mao who soon afterwards became, in the summer of 1920, as he states in his autobiography, "in theory and to some extent in action, a Marxist."[17]

Gandhi, on the other hand, was influenced in his childhood and youth by the deep religiosity of his illiterate mother and by the nonviolent Vaishnava culture of his family and neighbourhood including vegetarianism which always played an important role in his life and thought. Even during his student days in England (1888-1891), when he was trying to play the English gentleman with the help of Bond Street clothes and French, violin and elocution lessons, he not only retained his commitment to vegetarianism (he had vowed to his mother to remain a vegetarian while in England), but became an enthusiastic member of a vegetarian movement which brought him in contact with Western anarchist thought. The Hindu Brahmanical tradition in India justified war among the Kshatriyas, and Indian epics as well as ancient Indian history bear witness to considerable warfare among the Hindu kings; but Gandhi rejected this tradition and was drawn more to the nonviolent tradition of Buddhism, Jainism and Vaishnavism. He was influenced by the Ramayana, the Mahabharata and the Gita, but unlike the Hindu political extremists who saw in these classics a justification and apocalyptic vision of the violent destruction of the forces of Evil by the forces of Good, he interpreted the central theme of these classics as a conflict between good and evil within the human mind, in which good would eventually triumph through man's moral efforts. In fact he wrote a nonviolent interpretation of the Gita, popularly known as the *Gandhi Gita*. He was reasonably well read in Western history and thought, but remained unimpressed by the history of wars and revolutions and such contemporary ideological trends as Social Darwinism. The West influenced him in his youth through the New Testament, Plato's *Death of Socrates*,

and such pacifist anarchists as Tolstoy, Ruskin and the later Kropotkin (he also read and appreciated Thoreau, but only after he had
already developed and applied the technique of satyagraha in South
Africa). He read something of Marx, Engels, Lenin and Stalin for
the first time in 1944, at the age of seventy-five, and remained quite
unimpressed by what he read.[18]

The interaction of the minds and personalities of Mao and Gandhi
with the objective historical conditions in which they found themselves was crucial to the formation of their ideological perspectives
and the programmes and methods of action advocated by them. This
interaction, moreover, was not a static one, for the historical conditions changed over time, in some respects slowly and imperceptively,
in others quickly and radically, partly due to the movements led by
them and partly due to external causes; and the unfolding historical
drama in turn affected the political perspectives, programmes and
methods of the leaders and their movements. The ideologies and programmes of Mao and Gandhi, therefore, developed pragmatically
and dynamically over the course of their political career. It is to a
brief analysis of this development and its significance for the transformation of the two Asian countries that we now turn.

CHAPTER TWO

IDEOLOGICAL PERSPECTIVES

THE IDEOLOGICAL PERSPECTIVES of Mao Tse-tung and Gandhi are both highly charged with values. Mao, following Marx, regards the true consummation of liberty, equality and fraternity as the ultimate goal of social transformation. In Marxist thought liberty, equality and fraternity are relative values which in a class society are enjoyed only by the exploiting classes. The realization of these values by the masses of exploited and alienated people is contingent upon the emergence of a "human society or socialized humanity" in place of the "civil society," as Marx emphasized in his tenth thesis on Feuerbach. The socialization of humanity results step by step from the elimination of the contradiction between the forces of production and the relations of production through revolution, dictatorship of the proletariat and social ownership of the means of production. The socialization of production, according to Marx and Engels, represents the transition from necessity to freedom for humanity as a whole. It makes man the master of his social organization and environment, the struggle for existence ceases, and man becomes for the first time "the real, conscious Lord of Nature," as Engels wrote in *Socialism: Utopian and Scientific.* The socialization of production thus marks, in Engels' words, "the ascent of man from the kingdom of necessity to the kingdom of freedom." True equality is also, according to Marx, contingent on the socialization of production, because the distribution of the means of consumption, in his view, is a corollary of the distribution of the means of production, as he explained in his *Critique of the Gotha Programme.* In the first phase of Communist society, of course, the right of equality is a "right of inequality, in its content, like every right," on account of unequal individual endowments. Only in the higher phase of Communism would perfect equality be established on the basis of the principle:

2

from each according to his ability, to each according to his needs. Similarly, true human fraternity, according to Marx, is a corollary of the socialization of production. All social conflicts are fundamentally caused by class contradictions; and the socialization of production, by laying the foundations for a classless society and removing the alienation of the masses of working people, clears away the principal obstacle to human fraternity. The struggle for existence among men is replaced by the united struggle of a fraternal humanity against nature. The withering away of the state is merely an external symptom of the new inner social harmony. As is well known, Marx and Engels ridiculed the Feuerbachian theory of morals in which fraternity was treated as an absolute value independent of class divisions. Being a Marxist-Leninist, Mao naturally inherited this value-oriented approach of Marxism to social transformation. To take only one example, he has observed that the principal task of the Chinese people is "to build a new China of freedom and equality."[1] For the convenience of his people he has sometimes likened this socio-political goal to the Ta Tung or Great Harmony[2]—the classical Chinese utopia which would be characterized by liberty, equality and fraternity on the basis of the common ownership of wealth—although he had little respect for the religious texts in which this idea had been enunciated. But being a pragmatic political activist, he has never given a clear picture of China's ultimate destiny in terms of Marxism-Leninism.

Gandhi also geared his entire ideological thinking to the same ultimate values, although his values have deeper metaphysical moorings than those of Marxism-Leninism. His ultimate value-goal is Truth, which empirically means justice. This synthetic concept of justice consists, in the Gandhian scheme of values, of *ahimsa* or non-violence which to his mind is a wider name for fraternity, *swaraj* or liberty, both individual and collective, and *samata* or an inclusive equality. The task of social engineering, according to Gandhi, is the progressive instantiation of these values through the reconstruction of both individual and collective social life. The tools of social transformation devised by him are expected to perform a value-creating function and achieve, over a long period of time, a successive approximation to the ideal society in which the ultimate values would in theory be consummated, although he regarded all ultimate values as practically unattainable in their purity.[3]

This concern for ultimate values has inevitably injected a strong utopian element into both Marxism and Gandhism. But the classless, stateless and conflictless Marxian anarchist utopia, unlike that of Gandhi and other anarchists including Godwin, Tolstoy and Kropotkin, would have a highly developed technological and industrial base. Marx wanted the proletariat to seize and smash the political superstructure of capitalism but to preserve and further develop its industrial and technological infrastructure. The reorganization of the relations of production by the proletariat under social ownership was intended to remove the restraints on productive possibilities which the capitalistic relations of production had imposed on them, to free man through relentless technological progress from the struggle for existence, and to make available to the masses of people the leisure which Marx considered to be the "room for human development." The highly developed technological infrastructure of the Marxist utopia would also enable humanity to launch a Promethean struggle against the blind and wanton tyranny of nature. The Gandhian utopia, on the other hand, though stateless, classless, non-hierarchical and conflictless, would be agrarian, simple and self-sufficient, living in harmony with nature. Its horizontal organization would consist of oceanic circles of self-governing villages based on the barter system of exchange, agriculture and handicrafts, subsistence living, a high level of moral and spiritual well-being and a low level of technology and material well-being. Since the ultimate values would be consummated or instantiated in such a society, Gandhi called it *Ram Raj* (Kingdom of Heaven) in which there would be *sarvodaya* (equal development of all) and *poorna swaraj* (full freedom for all).[4]

But the extent of this divergence is considerably reduced when we move from Gandhi's utopia to his operational ideology. Gandhi was fully aware of the fact that his anarchistic utopia was only a utopia which represented more of an intellectual abstraction than a practicable social goal, more of a direction-indicator for purposes of social action than an immediately realizable social objective. He often likened it to the Euclidean point or straight line which exists only in theory but is nevertheless useful for solving the concrete problems of geometry.[5] The practical ideology which he developed in the course of his long political career grew largely out of the sociopolitical bases of the Indian freedom movement analysed in the first chapter, particularly by the ideological proclivities of the middle class intelligentsia which constituted his immediate following. Generally speaking, this intelligentsia was in favour of rapid industrialization and technological progress; and as the impact of the Russian Revolution and the industrialization of Russia was rapidly felt, most of its members, including Nehru, wanted not only quick industrialization but also an Indian form of socialism within the framework of political democracy. In Gandhi's practical ideology the economic system would be characterized by a good deal of complicated machinery and heavy industries, including heavy machinery for public utility works and the still heavier machinery required to produce them, electricity and the machinery implied by it, shipbuilding, ironworks, medicine-making, as well as heavy machinery for producing such relatively small machines as sewing machines, printing presses, surgical instruments, etc. He declared that some key industries were necessary, but refused to enumerate them. He also accepted railways, steamers and aeroplanes, and obviously also the heavy machinery and factories required to produce them.[6] Yet the difference between Marxism-Maoism and the operational ideology of Gandhi from this point of view is fundamental, one of kind rather than of degree. For Gandhi regarded all machinery as ideally undesirable and accepted a lot of it only as a necessary evil, and that also subject to the inalienable condition of maximum possible economic decentralization, with the economic reconstruction of the village as the nucleus.

Again, the teleological unfolding of the utopia in Marxism-Maoism, especially Maoism, has some formal similarities with that in the operational ideology of Gandhi. In Marxism the anarchist utopia unfolds itself first in the form of a dictatorship of the proletariat which involves a tremendous increase in the power of the state. By using this heightened state power dictatorially the proletariat is expected to destroy not only the exploiting classes, but also with them the apparatus of state power built by them supposedly only to oppress and exploit the underdog. With the occupation of the state as a mere instrument of exploitation gone, it withers away and transforms itself into the utopia. In Gandhi's operational ideology, too, the state is allowed not only to exist but also to increase its power and functions, especially economic functions. Here again it was the given historical and socio-political context and the conglomeration of forces in the Indian national movement that compelled

Gandhi to present a more authoritarian picture of the state and its functions than his purely private beliefs would have permitted. In his practical ideology not only would the government, parliament, armed forces, political parties and the rest of the paraphernalia of a modern state system exist, but the state must own or control all heavy and large-scale industries as well as large-scale employment. As early as 1924, seven years after the Russian Revolution and before a Communist Party was formally established in India, he made it quite clear that he was willing to accept a good deal of state ownership and control in the economic sphere. When it was pointed out to him that large-scale industries would be needed even to produce small machines like the Singer Sewing Machine of which he was a strong advocate, he at once observed: "But I am socialist enough to say that such factories should be nationalized or state-controlled. They ought to be working under the most attractive and ideal conditions, love taking the place of greed as motive. It is an alteration in the conditions of labour that I want."[7] He declared categorically in 1934 that although he regarded the state as ideally undesirable, state ownership of the means of production was, in his opinion, "better than private ownership."[8] He fully supported the programme of the nationalization of key industries adopted by the Indian National Congress at Karachi in 1931. He wrote in 1937 that "heavy machinery for work of public utility which cannot be undertaken by human labour has its inevitable place, but all that would be owned by the state and used entirely for the benefit of the people."[9] When the Indian National Congress set up a National Planning Committee in 1938, he cooperated with its efforts. In 1940 he supported the economic programme prepared by Jayaprakash Narayan which stated: "All large-scale collective production shall be eventually brought under collective ownership and control, and in this behalf the state shall begin by nationalizing heavy transport, shipping, mining and the heavy industries. . . . In all state-owned and state-managed enterprises, the workers shall be represented in the management through their elected representatives, and shall have an equal share in it with the representatives of the government."[10] Two years before his assassination he further expressed his views on state ownership in the following words: "Hence, without having to enumerate the key industries, I would have the state ownership where a large number of people have to work together. The ownership of the products of their labour, whether skilled or unskilled, will vest in them through the state."[11] Subsequently he added that "the state would look after secular welfare, health, communications, foreign relations, currency and so on,"[12] and even that "in the nonviolent order of the future, the land would belong to the state."[13] On several other occasions he also envisaged the possibility of cooperative farming by the peasants, subject to state ownership of land, although he did not develop the idea.[14] In 1944 a "Gandhian Plan" was prepared by an economist and approved by Gandhi. In it the development of heavy industries, including defence, heavy engineering, ships, locomotives, aircraft, mining, metallurgy and heavy chemicals were to take place in the public sector, while consumer goods were to be developed primarily through cottage industries. Existing private enterprises in the sector of heavy industries were to be purchased outright or brought under strict state control. All foreign enterprises were to be gradually purchased by the state. Perhaps most important of all, land was to be nationalized.[15]

But apart from the fundamental differences between the tools to be used by Marx and Gandhi for what Karl Popper has called "utopian engineering" (and which I shall discuss presently), the time-scales on which the two thinkers visualize the transformation of the newly powerful state into the utopia are quite different, and in this respect it is the Maoist rather than the Marxian view of historical dynamics which is comparable to that of Gandhi. After the victory of the proletarian revolution and the socialization of means of production, the state, Marx and Engels believed, would wither away in the not too distant future. As Engels explained in *Socialism: Utopian and Scientific*: "The first act by virtue of which the state really constitutes itself the representative of the whole society—the taking possession of the means of production in the name of society—that is, at the same time, its last independent act as a state. State interference in social relations becomes, in one domain after another, superfluous, and then dies out of itself; the government of persons is replaced by the administration of things, and by the conduct of the processes of production. The state is not 'abolished.' It dies out."[16] Gandhi, on the other hand, visualized a gradual, continuous and virtually perennial process of social transformation towards the distant utopia. He shared with Marx the grand vision of a utopian society but not Marx's belief in a sudden and quick method of bringing it into existence. "A few thousand years," he said, "are but a speck in the vast time circle. Someone has to make a beginning with a faith that will not flinch."[17]

It was Mao who brought the Marxian historical dynamics close to the time-scale visualized by Gandhi, no doubt due to his prolonged revolutionary experience in the opposition, his experience of exercising power for the transformation of China and his study of Soviet political development. An official pamphlet published in Peking in 1964 says that "For a very long period after the proletariat takes power, class struggle continues as an objective law independent of man's will, differing only in form from what it was before the taking of power." The main reason is explained as follows: "The socialist revolution on the economic front (in the ownership of the means of production) is insufficient by itself and cannot be consolidated. There must also be a thorough socialist revolution on the political and ideological fronts. Here a very long period of time is needed to decide 'who will win' in the struggle between socialism and capitalism. Several decades won't do it; success requires anywhere from one to several centuries." It is categorically stated that serious class contradictions exist in both China and the Soviet Union, and that both Stalin and Khrushchev had failed to understand the significance of these contradictions. Stalin had made a grave mistake when he "prematurely declared after agriculture was basically collectivized that there were 'no longer antagonistic classes' in the Soviet Union and that it was 'free of class conflicts';" and Khrushchev made an even graver mistake by declaring at the 22nd Congress of the CPSU that the Soviet Union had become "a state of the whole people" and that the CPSU had become "a party of the whole people." The fact is that, so runs the argument, "Throughout the stage of socialism the class struggle between the proletariat and the bourgeoisie in the political, economic, ideological and cultural and educational fields cannot be stopped. It is a protracted, repeated, tortuous and complex struggle. Like the waves of the sea it sometimes rises high and sometimes subsides, is now fairly calm and now very turbulent. It is a struggle that decides the fate of a socialist society." The upshot of the whole argument is that "it is necessary for all socialist countries to uphold the dictatorship of the proletariat" for an indefinitely long period of time, and that "as the vanguard of the proletariat, the Communist Party must exist as long as the dictatorship of the proletariat exists."[18] In other words, Mao has provided a rationalization for the continued existence of the dictatorship of the proletariat and the state ruled by this dictatorship purely in terms of internal necessity as distinct from the external threat of imperialism emphasized by Lenin and Stalin. In another essay on the *Historical Experience of the Dictatorship of the Proletariat* Mao went even further and observed: "The contradictions in various societies differ in character, as do forms of their solution, but society at all times develops through continual contradictions. Socialist society also develops through contradictions between the productive forces and the conditions of production. In a socialist or communist society, technical innovations and improvement in the social system inevitably continue to take place. . . . Humanity is still in its youth. The road it has yet to traverse will be no one knows how many times longer than the road it has already travelled. . . . One contradiction will lead to another, and when old contradictions are solved, new ones will arise. . . even when a communist society is established. Hence there will still be struggle between people, though its nature and form will be different from those in class societies."[19]

But the indefinite prolongation of the period, in the ideologies of Mao and Gandhi, during which the state transforms itself into statelessness does not answer the question how power would evaporate into powerlessness. Proudhon and Bakunin had disagreed with Marx on this point and argued that to set up a dictatorship of the proletariat on the morrow of the revolution was a wrong way to go about the creation of an anarchist society, since the dictatorship, instead of being transitional, would tend to perpetuate itself and lead to a growing accretion of power to the state. Gandhi was formulating his ideology in the context of a politically subject nation, and his programme of state ownership and control of key sectors of the economy was meant to apply to India immediately after independence. But he upheld the anarchist utopia till the last days of his life, and hence the logical connection between the operational ideology and the utopia in his thought is as important as that in Marxism-Maoism. Nor is this as purely academic a problem as it may sound, for the teleological link between the ideology and the utopia is a decisive factor in the direction of the entire process of social development; and this leads us to the problem of the tools of utopian engineering which have been built into the two ideologies concerned.

There is a common dialectical element in the Marxist-Maoist and Gandhian approaches to social transformation, which is also more pregnant in either case with a social content than Hegelian dialectics (although Marx and Mao would consider it impossible for a philosophical idealist like Gandhi to have a dialectical view of history with a social content). In Marxist theory contradictions are resolved by the dialectical process of negation of the negation and the restoration of the whole on a new and higher level of synthesis. As Engels explained in *Anti-Duhring*: "All Indo-Germanic people began with *common* property. Among almost all of them it was abolished, *negated*, in the course of social development, extended by other forms —private property, feudal property, etc. To negate this negation, to restore common property on a higher plane of development, is the task of the social revolution. Or: the philosophy of antiquity was spontaneous materialism. The latter gave rise to idealism, spiritualism, negation of materialism, first in the shape of the antithesis of soul and body, then in the doctrine of immortality and in monotheism. This spiritualism was universally disseminated through the medium of Christianity. The negation of this negation is the reproduction of the old on a higher plane, modern materialism, which in contrast with the past, finds its theoretical conclusion in scientific socialism."[20] Mao has further developed this theme in his famous essay *On Contradiction* where he argues that the violent seizure of state power and the establishment of the dictatorship of the proletariat, the building up of a strong Communist Party, armed insurrection and war are all negations of negations paving the way for a new synthesis. In his own words: "To consolidate the dictatorship of the proletariat or the dictatorship of the people is in fact to prepare the conditions for abolishing this dictatorship and advancing to the higher stage when all state systems are eliminated. To establish and build the Communist Party is in fact to prepare the conditions for the elimination of the Communist Party and all political parties. To build a revolutionary army under the leadership of the Communist Party and to carry on revolutionary war is in fact to prepare the conditions for the permanent elimination of war. These opposites are at the same time complementary."[21]

The Gandhian dialectic of social transformation is also based on the idea of negation of a negation, although he did not express it in this particular terminology. During the Noncooperation Movement

(1920-22), which was the first Gandhian mass movement against British rule in India, Rabindranath Tagore (who had received the Nobel Prize for literature in 1913 and became famous as a poet and thinker) criticized Gandhi for what he considered to be the negative character of the movement. India, he said, had always declared unity to be truth and separateness to be untruth. This unity "is that which comprehends all and, therefore, can never be reached through the path of negation." Gandhi replied that the existing relationship between Britain and India was an unequal and forcibly imposed relationship which itself was a negation. Real unity could be established on a positive basis only when the negative relationship involved in the imperialistic connection was ended and a voluntary relationship reestablished on the basis of freedom and equality. Rejection of the untruth, he argued, was necessary for the vindication of truth.[22] What applied, moreover, to relations between India and Britain also applied to class relations in India. Gandhi was deeply distressed by the inequality and exploitation which characterized the society around him, and regarded the negation of this negation as one of his major social objectives. The conflict between labour and capital, he believed, could not be resolved without eradicating the inequality between the two. In general, he argued: "A nonviolent system of government is clearly an impossibility so long as the wide gulf between the rich and the hungry millions persists. The contrast between the palaces of New Delhi and the miserable hovels of the poor labouring class nearby cannot last one day in a free India in which the poor will enjoy the same power as the richest in the land."[23] He advised the landlords and capitalists to accept his scheme of trusteeship under which the latter were to reduce themselves to poverty and live at the same economic and social level as the peasants and workers, drawing only a small commission for performing a managerial function. But if they did not yield to persuasion, which he considered highly probable, the remedy suggested by him was nonviolent non-cooperation and civil disobedience on the part of the peasants and workers.[24]

Thus the difference between the Maoist and Gandhian social dialectics is not one of form, but of content. According to Mao, contradictions are of two kinds, namely, contradictions between the people and their enemies and contradictions among the people. The first kind of contradiction is antagonistic, the second non-antagonistic.

For example, the contradictions between the proletariat and the bourgeoisie, between the peasantry and the feudal lords, and between the colonies and the imperialistic powers are antagonistic, while those between the working class and the peasantry, among members of the Communist Party and between society and nature are non-antagonistic.[25] In other words, domestic contradictions which are rooted in class conflict and those between colonies and imperial powers are antagonistic, while other contradictions are generally of a non-antagonistic character. But whether a particular contradiction must be operationally regarded as antagonistic or non-antagonistic is also contingent on historically relative tactical considerations. For example, during the long Sino-Japanese war, the external contradiction between China and Japan became the principal and, therefore, antagonistic contradiction, and the class contradictions inside China became secondary and non-antagonistic, thus permitting the Chinese Communist Party to collaborate with the Kuomintang.[26] Similarly, Mao has developed the Leninist theme that contradictions in a pre-revolutionary class society are antagonistic while those in the post-revolutionary socialist society are non-antagonistic, to justify the pragmatic economic policies of the government which tolerated the existence of rich peasants and capitalists for several years after the revolution. In his own words: "Contradictions in a socialist society are fundamentally different from those in old societies, such as capitalist society. In capitalist society contradictions find expression in acute antagonisms and conflicts, in sharp class struggle; they cannot be resolved by the capitalist system and can only be resolved by socialist revolution. On the contrary, the case is different with contradictions in socialist society where they are not antagonistic and can be resolved one after another by the socialist system itself."[27] Another way of expressing the same idea would be to say that contradictions which are antagonistic when the Communist Party is in opposition become non-antagonistic after it seizes power.

The operational significance of the distinction between antagonistic and non-antagonistic contradictions is that the former can be resolved only through the use of armed force, while the latter may be resolved through organizational and agitational methods. The argument that class contradictions can be resolved only through violent revolutions is, of course, central to Marxism. All power being concentrated in the state, and the state being an instrument of exploitation in the hands of the bourgeoisie, so runs the Marxist argument, the proletariat, though numerically much superior to the former, has no alternative to the seizure of power through armed revolution. As early as 1921 Mao used this argument against Bertrand Russell who, during a tour of China, had suggested that Communism could be established without violence or dictatorship.[28] He gave a fuller and more vivid exposition of this view at the Sixth Plenum of the Central Committee of the Communist Party of China, where he said: "Every Communist must grasp the truth: 'political power grows out of the barrel of a gun.'... All things grow out of the barrel of a gun. According to the Marxist theory of the state, the army is the chief component of state power. Whoever wants to seize and retain state power must have a strong army. ... Yes, we are the advocates of the omnipotence of revolutionary war; that is good, not bad, it is Marxist. The guns of the Russian Communist Party created socialism. We shall create a democratic republic. Experience in the era of imperialism teaches us that it is only by the power of the gun that the working class and the labouring masses can defeat the armed bourgeoisie and the landlords; in this sense we may say that only with the gun can the whole world be transformed."[29] To emphasize the universality of this principle further, he added: "The seizure of power by armed force, the settlement of the issue by war, is the central task and highest form of revolution. This Marxist-Leninist principle of revolution holds good universally, for China and all other countries."[30]

Nevertheless, Mao drew pointed attention to the special characteristics of the Chinese situation which not only made revolutionary war immediately necessary in China, but also gave this war a special strategic and tactical character. Referring to the particular characteristics of China, Mao observed that unlike the capitalist countries China was a semi-colonial and semi-feudal country where the working class had no legal right to organize strikes and no parliament to make use of, and therefore the oppressed classes in China had to launch armed insurrection immediately without going through struggles within the legal processes, and the insurrection had to proceed from the countryside to the cities. In the capitalist countries, on the other hand, which were characterized by bourgeois democracy and national independence, Communist Parties, he argued, could go through prolonged legal and parliamentary struggles for strengthening their organization and preparing for the seizure of state power through armed revolution. Moreover, in the capitalist countries the insurrection should proceed from the cities to the countryside, not the other way about.[31] Explaining the historical character and significance of such armed revolution in China, Mao observed in 1938: "When imperialism is not making armed attacks on our country, the Communist Party either wages civil war jointly with the bourgeoisie against the warlords (lackeys of imperialism), as in 1924-27 in the wars in Kwantung Province and the Northern Expedition, or unites with the peasants and urban petit-bourgeoisie to wage civil war against the landlord class and the comprador bourgeoisie (also lackeys of imperialism), as in the War of Agrarian Revolution of 1927-36. When imperialism launches armed attacks on China, the Party unites all classes and strata in the country opposing the foreign aggressors to wage a national war against the foreign enemy, as it is doing in the present War of Resistance against Japan.... In China war is the main form of struggle and the army is the main form of organization. Other forms such as mass organization and mass struggle are also extremely important and indeed indispensable and in no circumstance to be overlooked, but their purpose is to serve the war."[32] As is well known, the name given by Mao to this kind of revolutionary warfare in China is "people's war"—a quasi-political warfare by peasant masses, theoretically under the hegemony of the proletariat—which we shall discuss in the next chapter.

As regards the resolution of non-antagonistic contradictions through organizational methods other than revolutionary war, Mao explained some of these methods when he said that "the contradiction between the working class and peasant class in socialist society is resolved by the method of collectivization and mechanization in agriculture; contradiction within the Communist Party is resolved by the method of criticism and self-criticism; the contradiction between society and nature is resolved by the method of developing the productive forces."[33] But these and various other such methods, including periodic mass campaigns of a general or specific nature, are in fact fundamentally related to what Mao calls the "mass line"—a major and revolutionary technique of mass mobilization under the leadership of the Communist Party for the political, economic and social transformation of the country—which will be the subject-matter of Chapter IV. According to Mao's own statement, as we have seen, the organizational methods broadly related to the mass line would be subsidiary to people's war during the pre-socialist period, i.e. when the Communist Party is in opposition, while they would be the basic instrument of social transformation in the post-revolutionary socialist period, i.e. when the Communist Party is in power. But people's war and the mass line are closely interconnected, both theoretically and organizationally, as we shall see in the next two chapters.

Gandhi, on the other hand, argued that no social contradictions are really antagonistic in the sense that truth or justice cannot be vindicated without one side violently suppressing and even exter-minating the other. In fact he believed that the suppression or anni-hilation of the opponent by direct or indirect violence would really perpetuate the contradiction instead of resolving it, since violence, in his opinion, constitutes not a negation but an affirmation of and a contribution to the negation represented by various forms of in-justice. "Those who seek to destroy men rather than their manners," he said, "adopt the latter and become worse than those whom they destroy under the mistaken belief that the manners will die with them. They do not know the root of the evil."[34] The argument follows logi-cally and inevitably from Gandhi's conviction, largely derived from the Hindu social tradition as embodied in the doctrine of *karma*, that the end, meaning the actual result of social action, is determined by the nature and quality of the action itself rather than by the motive of the doer. In *Hind Swaraj* (1909) he told the imaginary reader who was arguing in favour of the forcible overthrow of the British from India: "Your belief that there is no connection between the means and the end is a great mistake. Through that mistake even men who have been considered religious have committed grievous crimes. Your reasoning is the same as saying that we can get a rose by planting a noxious weed. . . . The means may be likened to a seed, the end to a tree. I am not likely to obtain the result flowing from the worship of God by laying myself prostrate before Satan. . . . We reap exactly as we sow."[35] On a much later occasion he used the same argument in the following words: "As the means, so the end. There is no veil of separation between means and end. . . . Realization of the goal is in exact proportion to that of the means. This is a proposition that admits of no exception."[36] He explained that his primary concern had always been the conservation and progressive use of the means, since he knew that the end would inevitably follow from them. He put the matter in a nutshell when he said: "Means and end are convertible in my philosophy of life."[37] Therefore, he did not believe that liberty, equality or fraternity could be achieved through violent methods. "True democracy or the *swaraj* of the masses," he argued, "can never come through untruthful and violent means, for the simple reason that the natural corollary to their use would be to remove all opposition through the suppression or extermination of the antagonists. That does not make for individual freedom. Individual freedom can have the fullest play only under a regime of unadulterated *ahimsa*."[38] Equality, similarly, could only be established through nonviolent means of social transformation, according to Gandhi, since violence would inevitably lead to tyranny and exploitation in one form or another. The "exploitation-free" society visualized by him could only be established, in his opinion, when "the supreme instrument of defending just rights lay within the grasp of the unarmed individual."[39] Finally, as regards fraternity, it was obvious to Gandhi that this ultimate value could be realized not through a multiplication of violent acts, but by taking a vertical leap into a confrontation of organized violence by organized nonviolence.

Gandhi's anarchistic suspicion of power went hand in hand with his rejection of violence and expressed itself in his approach to the resolution of contradictions. He viewed the resolution of social contradictions not as the establishment of the power of one group over another, which is the central point of the Maoist approach, but as the transformation of social relationships which in fact is the substance of his definition of politics. "A nonviolent revolution," he declared, "is not a programme of 'seizure of power,' but it is a programme of transformation of relationships." It is the transformation of both the elements in the contradiction, and, therefore, of the entire contradiction, rather than the elimination or liquidation of one element by the other, as in the Marxist-Maoist view of contradictions, which constitutes the essence of the social and political thought of Gandhi, and distinguishes it clearly from two other contemporary conflict theories, namely, Marxism and Social Darwinism (including its political heir, Fascism). Indeed, it is this transformation of social relationships which, as I have tried to show elsewhere, is the essence of Gandhi's definition of both religion and politics.[40]

Such was the view taken by Gandhi of the historically principal contradiction he had to deal with, namely, the contradiction between British imperialism and Indian nationalism, as well as of the class contradictions in Indian society which assumed secondary importance in the given historical situation of his lifetime. As regards the principal contradiction, India's noncooperation, he explained repeatedly, was neither with the British nation nor with the West; it was noncooperation with the system the British had established in India, and with the ending of British rule the relations between India and Britain would be transformed into a new level of respect and mutuality. The same principle applied to class contradictions about which he said: "What is needed is not the extinction of landlords and capitalists, but a transformation of the existing relationship between them and the masses into something healthier and purer."[41]

But Gandhi had to adapt his idealistic belief in nonviolence as a creed to the strategic compulsions of the historical situation in India, just as Mao had to adapt his Marxist ideological heritage to the strategic compulsions of the Chinese situation. For resolving the principal contradiction between India and Britain, therefore, he advocated nonviolence as the most practicable and efficacious policy rather than as a creed. In a letter to the Viceroy immediately before launching the Noncooperation Movement, he explained the rationale of nonviolence as a policy thus: "In European countries the condonation of such grievous wrongs as the Khilafat and the Punjab would have resulted in a bloody revolution by the people. They would have resisted at all costs national emasculation such as the said wrongs imply. But half of India is too weak to offer violent resistance and the other half is unwilling to do so. I have, therefore, ventured to suggest the remedy of noncooperation which enables those who wish to dissociate themselves from the government and which, if it is unattended by violence and undertaken in an orderly manner, must compel it to retrace its steps and undo the wrongs committed." A few days later he told Congressmen: "There is another remedy before the country—drawing of the sword. If that was possible, India would not have listened to the gospel of noncooperation." As regards those who would resort to violence, he observed: "So far as I know, they must perish without delivering themselves or the country from the wrong"—a statement which truly reflected the fate of the terrorist movement in India up to that time. He explained that personally he believed in "the conquest of physical might by spiritual strength," and would prefer the Indian people to fight the British empire with spiritual power. "However, being a practical man," he said, "I do not wait till India recognizes the practicability of the spiritual life in the political world. India considers herself to be powerless and paralysed before the machine-guns, the tanks and the aeroplanes of the English. And she takes up noncooperation out of her weakness. It must still serve the same purpose, namely, bring her delivery from the crushing weight of British injustice, if a sufficient number of people practise it."[42] The technique of political struggle and of social transformation which Gandhi thus adopted in India, as is well known, is satyagraha, which we shall discuss in the next chapter along with the people's war of Mao Tse-tung.

It was, therefore, natural that Gandhi would be fundamentally opposed to Communism as an ideology and to the Soviet system of government during his lifetime. As early as 1920 he declared that "India does not want Bolshevism."[43] While referring to the attempts of the Indian Communists to convert him to Communism, he wrote in 1924: "I am as yet ignorant of what Bolshevism is. I have not been able to study it. I do not know whether it is for the good of Russia in the long run. But I do know that in so far as it is based on violence and the denial of God, it repels me. I do not believe in short-violent-cuts to success. Those Bolshevik friends who are bestowing their attention on me should realize that however much I may sympathize with and admire worthy motives, I am an uncompromising opponent of violent methods even to serve the noblest of causes. There is, therefore, really no meeting ground between the school of violence and myself."[44] In a critical reference to Russia he observed three years later: ". . .from what I know of Bolshevism, it not only does not preclude the use of force, but freely sanctions it for the expropriation of private property and maintaining the collective ownership of the same. And if that is so, I have no hesitation in saying that the Bolshevik Government in its present form cannot last long. For it is my firm conviction that nothing enduring can be built on violence."[45] As regards the Russian system of state-controlled production and distribution, he observed that he would dote on it had it not been based on force.[46] The free and full development of the individual, he argued, was impossible under the dictatorial form of government prevalent in the Soviet Union. "As I look at Russia," he observed, "the life there does not appeal to me. . . . In modern times it is beneath human dignity to lose individuality and become a mere clog in the machine. I want every individual to become a full-blooded, fully developed member of society."[47] Referring to the ideal of equality advocated by the Communists, he stated that it would be readily acceptable to him in the abstract, but not in the concrete form in which it was found in the Soviet Union, since the violent method adopted by the Soviet Government for the establishment of economic equality was repugnant to him.[48] He was opposed to "Communism which is imposed on a people."[49] He accepted the Communist goal of a classless society, he said, since his own ideal was one of abolishing all social distinctions; but he did not believe in eradicating evil from the human breast at the point of a bayonet.[50] He doubted the claim of those who maintained that inequalities had been abolished in Russia, because he did not believe that equality could be established through violence.[51] So far as the broad achievements of the Soviet Union were concerned, Gandhi observed that while he would be the last man to minimize those achievements, he could not accept a structure based on force.[52] He further observed that voluntary co-operation would produce a social order vastly superior to that of the Soviet Union.[53] Rejecting the usual Marxist argument that the end justifies the means in connection with the Soviet system, he said: "Some say there is ruthlessness in Russia but that it is exercised for the lowest and the poorest and is good for that reason. For me there is very little good in it. Some day this ruthlessness will create an anarchy, worse than ever we have seen."[54] He summed up his own impression of the international significance of Soviet Communism when he wrote in 1938: "Russia has a dictator who dreams of peace and thinks he will wade to it through a sea of blood. No one can say what the Russian dictatorship will bring to the world."[55]

But Gandhi's quest for ultimate values made him equally critical of the two other ideologies of his time, namely, Fascism and Western capitalist democracy. He was totally opposed to the Nazi system of government on account of its being based on force. He believed that the German people had been unjustly treated by the great powers and that the Treaty of Versailles had been particularly unfair to them, but he condemned the reign of terror on which the Nazi regime was based. In his own words: "Germany is showing to the world how efficiently violence can be worked, when it is not hampered by any hypocrisy or weakness masquerading as humanitarianism. It is also

showing how hideous, terrible and terrifying it looks in its naked-
ness." About the Hitlerite tyranny he said: "The tyrants of old never
went so mad as Hitler seems to have gone. And he is doing it with
religious zeal. For he is propounding a new religion of exclusive and
militant nationalism in the name of which any inhumanity becomes
an act of humanity to be rewarded here and hereafter. The crime of
an obviously mad but intrepid youth is visiting upon his whole race
with unbelievable ferocity." So indignant was he at the persecution
of Jews in Germany that he went to the extent of saying that had he
believed in the method of war, he would have regarded a war against
Germany for the sake of humanity as fully justified.[56]

Gandhi was also fundamentally opposed to Western capitalist
democracy, because he felt that the industrialism on which this
system was based necessarily led to violence, oppression, exploitation, the concentration of wealth, imperialism and inequality, and
because he regarded the acquisitive character of this system as detrimental to the moral development of man. As early as 1926 he declared: "I fight capitalism. The West teaches us to avoid concentration
of capital."[57] He even argued, almost like Lenin, that capitalism
necessarily led to imperialism. The only difference between Gandhi
and Lenin in this respect lies in the fact that while Lenin considered
the relations of production characteristic of the capitalist economic
system rather than industrialism as such to be the cause of imperialism, Gandhi thought that the roots of imperialism lay in the unrestrained growth of machinery and the resultant industrialism.[58] As
regards the system of government prevalent in the Western countries,
Gandhi observed: "Democracy of the West is, in my opinion, only
so-called. It has germs in it, certainly, of the true type. But it can only
come when all violence is eschewed and malpractices disappear. The
two go hand-in-hand. Indeed, malpractice is a species of violence."[59]
The malpractices of the Western governments, according to Gandhi,
included not only direct resort to violence whenever the occasion
arose, but also imperialism, suppression of the freedom struggles of
the Asian and African nations, exploitation and oppression of the
coloured peoples, the concentration of capital, economic inequality,
etc. In 1940 he said to an American journalist: "Take your own case.
Your land is owned by a few capitalist owners. The same is true of
South Africa. These large holdings cannot be sustained except by
violence, veiled if not open. The Western democracy as it functions

today is diluted Nazism or Fascism. At best it is a mere cloak to hide the Nazi and Fascist tendencies of imperialism.... It was not through the democratic methods that Britain bagged India. What is the meaning of the South African democracy? Its very constitution has been drawn up to protect the white man against the coloured man, the natural occupant. Your own history is perhaps blacker still, in spite of what the Northern States did for the abolition of slavery. The way you have treated the Negro presents a discreditable record. And it is to save such democracies that the war is being fought. There is something very hypocritical about it."[60] He argued that there was no distinction between Nazism and the "double autocracy" which ruled India.[61] In 1942 he wrote to Louis Fischer: "I see no difference between the Fascist or Nazi powers and the Allies. All are exploiters, all resort to ruthlessness to the extent required to compass their end. America and Britain are very great nations, but their greatness will count as dust before the bar of dumb humanity, whether African or Asiatic.... They have no right to talk of human liberty and all else, unless they have washed their hands clean of the pollution.... Then, but not till then will they be fighting for a new order."[62]

Apalled by all the three ideological forms in which modern civilization appeared in his lifetime, namely, Western capitalist democracy, Communism and Fascism, Gandhi thus became strongly critical of the evils of *civilization*, almost in the same way in which Marx and Engels were critical of *the civilization* as they saw it. The *Hind Swaraj*, a booklet written by Gandhi in 1908, is a frontal attack on what he considered to be the evils of civilization, i.e. Western civilization; and in 1938, at the age of sixty-nine, he observed that he would not change anything he had written in it. By that time he had also witnessed the new civilizations represented by Soviet Communism and German Nazism.

It was for this reason that he said, in reply to the contention of the Indian Communists that the whole character of the Second World War had been transformed by Hitler's attack on the Soviet Union and the new front of the Allies: "Between Scylla and Charybdis, if I sail in either direction, I suffer shipwreck. Therefore, I have to be in the midst of the storm."[63] His criticism of industrial civilization was initially a reaction against imperialism, exploitation, concentration of wealth, inequality and other evils of Western capitalism. The Soviet system, which was based on an ideological rejection of the political and economic system of the West, but utterly repugnant to him due to the violence and dictatorship which characterized it, made him all the more sceptical of the theory that industrialism could be turned into a blessing by reorganizing the relations of production. Fascism further confirmed him in his suspicion of industrialism. He became increasingly convinced that no amount of social reorganization could possibly lead to the attainment of the ultimate values of nonviolence, freedom and equality, if industrialism itself was not restricted. This was, in fact, one of the major differences between him and Nehru. As Gandhi said in 1940: "Nehru wants industrialization because he thinks that if it is socialized, it would be free from the evils of capitalism. My own view is that the evils are inherent in industrialism, and no amount of socialization can eradicate them."[64]

Gandhi was, therefore, convinced that if violence, exploitation, tyranny and other forms of injustice were to be permanently eradicated, the infrastructure of a just society based on economic and political decentralization had to be constructed over a long period of time to replace unrestrained industrialism and the associate concentration of power. He thus linked satyagraha as a means of resolving contradictions to a massive but decentralized programme of constructive activity called the "constructive programme." Although he formulated a particular constructive programme for the given situation in India, it was in fact a general technique of social reorganization applicable to other situations as well. As in the case of the Maoist techniques of people's war and mass line, satyagraha and the constructive programme are closely interconnected, as we shall see in the next two chapters. Apart from the question of violence, a fundamental difference between the twin means of social transformation advocated by Mao and Gandhi respectively is that while people's war is primarily an instrument of the Communist Party for capturing power and is supposed to become redundant for domestic purposes once the Communist Party is in power, and the mass line emerges from secondary importance in the first phase to primary significance in the second, both satyagraha and the constructive programme, as understood by Gandhi, are perennial means of social transformation, irrespective of who runs the government. His distrust of power and violence made him fundamentally suspicious of all state systems, and he constantly declared that his main object was to free the Indian people not only from the British yoke but from any yoke whatsoever, that the Indian people should always remain prepared to fight against a brown tyranny or an Indian Rockefeller.

But there is a common third dimension to the ideological approaches of Mao Tse-tung and Gandhi, namely, their common emphasis on the transformation of the consciousness of the individual, which is crucial to their operational ideologies as well as to the teleological link between these ideologies and the utopias to which they are supposed to be related. Marx and Engels believed that the consciousness of the individual was a derivative of his class character as determined by the relations of production and that, therefore, this consciousness would more or less automatically undergo a transformation once production had been socialized and class contradictions eliminated. Socialist consciousness of the individual would follow from the socialization of the means of production. With Lenin the Party became the agent, as the vanguard of the proletariat, for removing the "false consciousness" of individuals both before and immediately after the revolution. In his *On Practice* Mao argued, on the basis of the Marxian theory of knowledge, that the revolutionary consciousness of the individual can be awakened only through his participation in the productive process. But subsequently he laid great stress, especially during the Cultural Revolution, on the revolutionary transformation of the consciousness of every individual, including the Communist Party cadres, through a personal moral effort involving much more than mere participation in the productive process. The *Quotations from Chairman Mao Tse-tung* can be interpreted as an exhortation of Party workers and the common people to revolutionize their individual consciousness in terms of Mao Tse-tung's thought. The heroes glorified during the Cultural Revolution were all common individuals who had a high degree of revolutionary consciousness. In his foreword to the *Quotations from Chairman Mao Tse-tung* Lin Piao observed that Mao's thought was "an inexhaustible source of strength and a spiritual atom bomb of infinite power."[65] Even in 1965, at least a year before the Cultural Revolution had started, Mao told Edgar Snow that unless the new generation, which had not participated in the Communist revolution, developed a new revolutionary consciousness, the wheels of history might move backwards.[66] During the Cultural Revolution Joan Robinson witnessed in China what she considered to be an attempt on the part of Mao to eliminate the ego of the individual.[67] Stuart Schram has observed that "Mao tends to exalt the revolutionary will of human beings until it becomes not merely an important factor in history, but an all-powerful force capable of reshaping the material environment in a completely arbitrary fashion."[68] Franz Schurmann has similarly argued that "*The Thought of Mao Tse-tung* stresses the importance of the ideological transformation of the individual," and that "what Mao hopes to achieve is such a spiritual transformation of man that the new revolutionary attitudes and behaviour will continue beyond his death." He has added that "given the mystery and intractability of human nature, regardless of race, colour, or creed, a scientific campaign to change the soul of man seems to be a task which normally only God would have set himself to accomplish."[69]

Gandhi regarded the control of the self-interest of the individual as an essential prerequisite to the transformation of social relationships in terms of the ultimate values. The values must be inculcated in the individual before they can find true social expression. Like Mao he regarded theory as inseparable from practice, and believed that through such organized social action as the constructive programme and satyagraha, the individual would be constantly trained to control his purely personal impulses. But he emphasized, unlike Marx, the need for a private moral effort on the part of the individual before he can qualify himself for social action. In order to engage in the task of transforming social relationships, the individual must observe, he said, the five vows enjoined by the ancient Indian scriptures, namely, *satya* (truth), *ahimsa* (positive nonviolence or love), *asteya* (non-stealing or non-exploitation), *aparigraha* (non-possession or non-acquisitiveness) and *brahmacharya* (control of animal passion). "Unless you impose on yourselves the five vows," he warned his workers, "you may not embark on the experiment at all."[70] The most important practical work which helps the individual to realize the ultimate values in their own lives, according to him, is "bread-labour," which an authority on Gandhi has described as "the first moral law of life" in Gandhian thought.[71] The principle of bread-labour, which Gandhi borrowed from Tolstoy (who in turn had got it from Bondaref), Ruskin, the Gita and the Bible, was defined by him as "the divine law that man must earn his bread by labouring with his own hands." It would eliminate exploitation as well as more direct forms of violence through a heightened social awareness; it would impart creative freedom to the individual and make him free of any external control, including that of the government; and by simplifying life and preventing the growth of the acquisitive spirit, it would lead to spontaneous economic equality. Hence, according to Gandhi: "Bread-labour is a veritable blessing to one who would observe nonviolence. . . ." He even went to the extent of saying that only a man or a woman who performed bodily labour to earn bread had a right to live, and that people engaged in intellectual pursuits were no exception. He pointed out, however, that since nine-tenths of the human race lives on manual labour anyway, the principle of bread-labour simply amounts to the compulsory performance of some manual labour on the part of the remaining one-tenth. In the given conditions of India of his time, he considered spinning to be an ideal form of bread-labour.[72] Thus Gandhi agreed with Mao that participation in productive labour is the most important and effective way of achieving this transformation. The major difference between their ideas on the subject is that while the transformation of individual consciousness advocated by Mao is primarily a process of political self-education, that insisted on by Gandhi has a quasi-religious character—a fact which may be explained not only in terms of the Marxist atheism of Mao and the private religiosity of Gandhi, but also by a certain sociological factor in the given situation discussed in the first chapter, namely, the relatively atheistic character of the Chinese cultural tradition and the deeply religious character of the Indian.

It is obvious that the kind of social transformation both Mao and Gandhi have in view cannot be called "modernization," if the term means either Westernization or the building of the political, economic and military infrastructure of state power. Both of them have been strongly opposed to the political and economic systems of the West, which they have considered to be basically detrimental to the realization of the ultimate values of liberty, equality and fraternity, and have tried to devise alternative systems for the emancipation of their peoples and the progressive realization of these values. As regards the power interpretation of modernization, there are strong anarchistic and populist elements not only in the utopias but also in the operational ideologies of both Mao and Gandhi which tend to go against this interpretation. Only if modernization is defined as a value-oriented and multi-dimensional process of political, economic and socio-cultural innovation, can one speak of their ideological perspectives in terms of modernization. But whether we characterize them as ideologies of modernization or not, the crucial question is whether and to what extent the methods by which the Maoist and Gandhian states are brought into existence, sustained and propelled towards the ultimate values, do in fact lead to a progressive realization of these values in social and political life by successive approximation, and if not, what other consequences they may be logically expected to lead to. In other words, a comparative analytical and historical study of the Maoist innovations of people's war and mass line with the Gandhian innovations of satyagraha and the constructive programme, as well as of the state systems within which these are expected to operate, would be necessary in order to make an overall comparative assessment of the social technology involved in the two ideologies. Prima facie, the basis of people's war in military strength no less than in mass mobilization, the military and industrial power which is expected to sustain the socialist state, and the admittedly doctrinaire and dictatorial though broad-based one-party system which would govern it, would together establish a very powerful state system which Gandhi found repugnant to the common ultimate values cherished by Mao and himself; and according to Mao, this kind of state will continue to exist for a very long and indefinite period of time, at least for several centuries. Apparently, the mass line is the only technique by which Mao expects this state to transform itself very slowly in the very long run. Prima facie also, the means Gandhi adopted for bringing the Indian state into existence, namely, mass satyagraha, the democratic and essentially decentralized character of the state visualized by him in spite of considerable state control, and the general and perennial character of satyagraha and the constructive programme irrespective of forms of government, all indicate a state system with a relatively weak power structure (in the sense of military and industrial power) progressively weakening further with the passage of time, and therefore more consistent with the realization of the anarchist utopia. But whether such a state would be able to defend its external sovereignty in a real contemporary world, and whether the ultimate values cherished by Gandhi would truly be consummated in the kind of anarchist society he has in mind, are questions whose answers are contingent upon the efficacy or otherwise of the social technology and state structure visual-

ized by him as compared to those visualized by Mao, which in turn
has to be ascertained by both logical analysis and empirical verifica-
tion as far as practicable. It is to this problem, then, that we address
ourselves in the next three chapters.

CHAPTER THREE

PEOPLE'S WAR AND SATYAGRAHA

BOTH PEOPLE'S WAR and mass satyagraha have a highly political character. One of the fundamental principles on which people's war is based, namely, that war is a continuation of politics by other means, was first forcefully enunciated by Clauswitz, later borrowed from him by Lenin, and finally developed by Mao. "War is politics with bloodshed," wrote Mao in one of his celebrated military essays, and therefore, "a national revolutionary war as great as ours cannot be won without universal and thoroughgoing political mobilization."[1] In other words, people's war is a war waged by politically organized masses, rather than by a standing army on behalf of the masses. It is a theme which has been endlessly repeated by him in all his military writings during all phases of his revolutionary career. Naturally, such a politically organized war by the masses requires a high level of political consciousness on their part, and this is why Mao's emphasis on the revolutionary transformation of the individual consciousness assumes major importance for the revolutionary endeavour. Undoubtedly, the reliance on the masses for fighting the revolutionary war was an outgrowth, in the given Chinese context, of the relative inferiority of the revolutionary forces in regard to arms. As Mao argued: "The mobilization of the common people throughout the country will create a vast sea in which to drown the enemy, create the conditions that will make up for our inferiority in arms and other things and create the prerequisite for overcoming every difficulty in the war."[2] Mao's belief in the great power of the revolutionary consciousness of the people has led him to insist that they rather than weapons decide the issue of victory or defeat in a war. In his opinion, "weapons are an important factor in war, but not the decisive factor; it is people, not things, that are decisive."[3] Lin Piao ably summed up this basic principle in the formula: "You rely on modern weapons and we rely on highly conscious revolutionary people."[4] The same is essentially true of mass satyagraha also, more so because of its inalienably nonviolent character. Gandhi advocated mass satyagraha as a means for ending British rule in India, as we have seen, partly on account of the weakness and demoralization of the Indian people in the face of the infinitely superior armed strength of the British, and his belief that a violent attempt to overthrow British rule in India in the given situation would be utterly futile. He, therefore, had to rely solely on the organized political power of the Indian masses and hence to lay great stress on the transformation of the individual consciousness. Only the discipline required of the masses by Gandhi for the transformation of their political and social outlook was moral and quasi-religious, as opposed to the purely political and military discipline advocated by Mao.

It follows that both people's war and satyagraha must be based on the broadest possible common front of the masses. Ever since Mao assumed command of the CCP, he tried to unite as many sections of people as possible in a broad revolutionary front. The general historical experience of Western imperialism on the part of the Chinese people, and the prolonged Japanese occupation in particular made the establishment of such a united front a relatively easy task, as I have pointed out in the first chapter, but even in the earlier and later phases of the revolution made by him Mao tried to keep class contradictions in the Communist-controlled areas at a relatively nonantagonistic level. In his military writings he has constantly emphasized the vital importance of building the widest possible front of the revolutionaries for the success of a people's war, and Lin Piao described it as a basic strategy of such wars.[5] Mass satyagraha in India also required, as I pointed out earlier, the policy of a united front, although Gandhi did not call it by that name. He continually stressed the need for national unity, allowed an amazing diversity of views to exist within the broad platform of the Indian National Congress, systematically worked against such divisive social forces as untouchability and communalism, and deliberately avoided any radical class or caste conflict on a national scale during the freedom movement. Indeed, it is difficult to see how the kind of national resistance involved in people's war and mass satyagraha can be organized effectively in the absence of an undivided popular front.

But since people's war in China and mass satyagraha in India took place in a primarily agrarian context, the most important organizational requirement for both was the political mobilization of the peasantry. Marx and Engels had visualized the socialist revolution only in a mature capitalist country, after the forces of production had more or less reached the limit of their quantitative growth within the system. Moreover, they regarded the peasantry as a property-oriented and relatively reactionary class which could not be expected to act as the vanguard of the revolution. The socialist revolution envisaged by them was essentially a proletarian revolution. Although they often underlined the importance of studying the objective conditions of a given society from the point of view of the feasibility of a proletarian revolution, and although there is some controversy as to whether Marx had developed a theory of the "Asiatic mode of production," there can be very little doubt that he regarded the capitalist transformation of Asiatic societies as an inalienable prerequisite to a revolution in these societies. Lenin considered the objective conditions in the predominantly agricultural Asiatic societies to be suitable for armed revolutions even before such revolutions could be expected in the advanced capitalist countries. But Lenin was speaking only of a possibility and thought, moreover, that a peasant revolution could develop in Asia only with the help of the international proletariat. But in the given socio-economic condition of China the peasantry was the only possible mass base for the revolution, and Mao had the courage to look this massive reality in the face and take it with both hands to make the revolution. From 1927 onwards he had practically no doubt left in his mind regarding the feasibility and desirability of a peasant revolution in China. Although he occasionally referred to the need for the proletarian leadership of the peasant revolution, this was more in the nature of a theoretical concession to Marxism-Leninism and an emphasis on the revolutionary potentiality of the rural proletariat, than a characterization of the revolution as it actually developed in China under his leadership. It was this peasant base and essentially agrarian character of the Maoist revolution that impelled Mao to innovate the transitional ideology of the "new democratic revolution," in which the emphasis was on the broad alliance of the masses rather than on the leadership of the proletariat, and to name the government which came to power in 1949 as the "people's democratic dictatorship" rather than dictatorship of the proletariat (Marxism-Leninism visualizes only two stages of the revolution: the bourgeois-democratic revolution which marks the transition between feudalism and capitalism—Sun Yat-sen's revolution having been identified as such by Lenin, Stalin and Mao—and the proletarian revolution which ends capitalism and establishes socialism under the dictatorship of the proletariat). Mao has argued that the successful self-identification of the Communist Party with the peasant masses and the failure of the Kuomintang in this respect was the principal cause of the success of the Communist revolution in China.[6] This self-identification of the Communist Party with the peasantry was no doubt facilitated by the insurrectionary tradition of the Chinese peasantry referred to in the first chapter. As Barrington Moore and others have pointed out, the Communist Party was in a sense heir to the past peasant rebellions of China, the Kuomintang to the mandarins.[7] Gandhi also had to base his entire political movement in India primarily on peasant power, as is generally well known. Although the mass satyagrahas led by him included many cities as well, they were primarily agrarian movements involving the vast peasant masses of India. And it was his ability to identify the national movement led by the Indian National Congress with the peasantry, which neither the Moderates nor the Extremists within the Congress had been able to do before his entry into Indian politics, that imparted to the movement a mass character and an irresistible political power.

The peasant character of people's war and satyagraha logically led to the building of the organizational nucleus of both the forms of struggle in rural base areas. Mao always regarded the building of the base areas in the countryside as the most important task of the Communist Party during the period when it was in opposition, and the entire strategy of the armed revolution led by him was to consolidate these rural base areas and then to encircle and capture the cities from these areas. The building of a base area primarily means bringing a certain area under the political, military and administrative control of the Communist Party, introducing preliminary land reforms there, helping the people in their daily lives with welfare activities, indoctrinating them politically, arming as large a section of them as possible, and establishing an emotional identity between the people and the party and its fighting forces, so that the guerillas in the base areas can live and work among the people there like fish swimming in water, as Mao once said. These areas are then used not only as bases of military operations, but also as the terminal points of dispersal where the actual soldiers can no longer be traced. The transformation of the villages into armed bases of the revolution has the strategic advantage that the enemy is deprived of any major and visible target whose capture would bring victory, and is faced instead with a diffused mass of ordinary people who, though not in uniform, are operationally indistinguishable from the soldiers. The successful building of base areas in the countryside is thus closely interconnected with and heavily dependent on the implementation of the mass line and the virtual obliteration of the distinction between the organizational and military functions of the party cadres. It is also vitally important for the consolidation of the base areas and the success of people's war, as Mao often emphasized, that the army should produce its own requirements, including all possible arms and ammunition, since the revolutionary rural bases would be necessarily cut off from the sources of supply in the cities. The basic strategy was the same in the case of the mass satyagrahas in India. After the incidence of violence at the village of Chauri Chaura in February 1922 which impelled Gandhi to call off the noncooperation movement immediately, he realized the urgent need for building organizational units in the rural areas, and for the next eight years devoted most of his energies to this task. The centres of constructive work which thus grew up all over village India performed essentially the same function of mobilization and political consolidation of the rural areas as the Maoist base areas did in China. These centres not only recruited and trained a volunteer cadre in the area, but also devoted themselves to the task of village development, political education of the villagers, and establishing an emotional identity between the village people and the cadre of freedom fighters, generally belonging to the Indian National Congress. Moreover, like Mao's party cadres, the Gandhian workers were constantly engaged in productive activities in the form of agriculture, cottage industries and handicrafts, so that they could be self-reliant as far as possible and thus free from government control or occupational obligations in times of struggle. And as in the case of the Communist base areas, the distinction between the cadre of constructive workers and the satyagrahis during a struggle was virtually obliterated; the same people who normally assumed the responsibility for constructive work turned into satyagrahis when the call was given for satyagraha. A satyagrahi, as Gandhi used to say, must always be in one of three possible conditions: engaged in constructive work, engaged in satyagraha, or in prison.[8] The organizational link between the constructive work centres and satyagraha was very close, and as Joan V. Bondurant has pointed out, the success of a particular satyagraha was often in direct proportion to the organizational strength of the constructive programme.[9] Usually Gandhi did not give a call for even a local satyagraha unless there was a substantial network of constructive work centres in the area.

These compulsions of a rural society were not, however, considered by either Mao or Gandhi to be a serious constraint on the universal applicability of people's war and satyagraha respectively. Both felt not only that people's war and satyagraha could be successfully used against national governments as well as against foreign aggression, but also that this was true of the whole world, irrespective of historical circumstances. In this respect, however, the ideas of both evolved considerably over time. Until 1949 Mao seemed to argue that people's war was possible only in a vast, populous, predominantly agrarian and semi-colonial country which, moreover, had a strong Communist Party. In particular he attached great importance to the vast territory and population of China which, he argued, made mobile and protracted warfare and concentration of numerically superior forces possible. He specifically mentioned Belgium and Abyssinia as countries where people's war would not be possible. The predominantly agricultural character made possible the building of remote base areas in the villages outside the easy reach of the organized armed forces of the government and enabled the revolutionary forces to consolidate their strength until they were ready to encircle and capture the cities. The semi-colonial character of the country helped to isolate and divide the ruling party. The presence of a strong Communist Party made possible the mobilization and consolidation of the revolutionary sections of the people. It was for these reasons that Mao predicted the ultimate victory of the Communist Party over the Kuomintang as well as the victory of China over Japan in the protracted anti-Japanese war.[10] India, Mao has argued consistently even after 1949, is another country where these conditions are largely present—a theme that has been vigorously pursued in recent years by Chinese newspapers, journals and foreign radio broadcasts which have also called for an armed revolution in India and promised all help to it.[11] But although such conditions are still regarded as particularly propitious for people's war, since the beginning of the Sino-Soviet conflict, and particularly during the last decade or so, Mao and his followers have relaxed the conditions under which people's war was originally considered possible. The relative success of the protracted people's war in Vietnam and the revolutionary freedom movement in Algeria were probably partly responsible for this optimism. In the late 'fifties Mao developed the famous thesis that the whole of Asia, Africa and Latin America constituted the "rural areas of the world" and were ripe for people's war. From there the world revolution would grow, encircle and capture the "cities of the world" consisting mainly of the North American and West European states. In 1965 Lin Piao stated in his celebrated essay on people's war that while such war was necessary "for the present revolutionary struggles of all oppressed nations and peoples," it was so "particularly for the revolutionary struggles of the oppressed nations and peoples of Asia, Africa and Latin America against imperialism and its lackeys," because "since World War II the proletarian revolution has for various reasons been temporarily held back in North American and West European countries." The main consideration for the success of people's war now seemed to be the agricultural character of a country. Lin referred to the similarity of agricultural conditions between the Asian, African and Latin American countries on the one hand and pre-revolutionary China on the other, and observed that it was precisely for this reason that Mao's theory of building base areas in the countryside for encircling the cities was not only suitable for these continents, but was in fact attracting a lot of attention there. He repeated Mao's theme that the people of Asia, Africa and Latin America must not only liberate themselves by people's war, but must also encircle and defeat industrialized North America and West Europe.[12] From the period of the Cultural Revolution, however, the conditions for the success of people's war were relaxed even further to include practically the whole world. "People's war," said a *Renmin Ribao* editorial in 1967, "is a powerful weapon for transforming the world. So long as they grasp the great weapon of Chairman Mao's theory of people's war, the revolutionary people of the whole world will be able to make themselves invincible and wipe out all such monsters as imperialism, modern revisionism and

4

the reactionaries of all countries."[13] Finally, in 1970 Mao saw the vision of people's war engulfing the whole world. In a statement in May that year he noted that "Nixon's fascist atrocities have kindled the raging flames of the revolutionary mass movement in the United States," and that "the revolutionary struggles of the peoples of North America, Europe and Oceania are all developing vigorously." As during the Cultural Revolution, he now attached primary significance to revolutionary consciousness rather than to environmental conditions. Contrary to his earlier observations regarding the conditions necessary for the success of a people's war, he now emphatically declared: "A weak nation can defeat a strong, a small nation can defeat a big. The people of a small country can certainly defeat aggression by a big country, if only they dare to rise in struggle, dare to take up arms and grasp in their own hands the destiny of their own country. This is a law of history."[14]

Gandhi, too, initially conducted his experiments in satyagraha in South Africa in special historical conditions. He organized and led in satyagraha a relatively small and compact community of Indians against a white government which, though autocratic and racist, functioned within a legal and constitutional framework. The ethnocentric solidarity of the community led by him, the form and character of the white government, and the limited nature of the demands which were concerned with marginal relief from racial and economic injustice, all probably contributed to the relative success of the experiments. In India, too, he carried on his experiments with satyagraha, including the two national mass satyagrahas of 1920-22 and 1930-33 and numerous local satyagrahas, in the historically given conditions analysed before. Nor did he concern himself with the prospects of satyagraha in other parts of the world, or against foreign aggression in India and elsewhere, until the late 'thirties. In fact he had supported the British war effort in the First World War and even tried to help the recruitment of soldiers in India without much success. It was immediately before, during and after the Second World War that Gandhi expressed himself forcefully in favour of satyagraha in other parts of the world. He advised the Jews of Germany to rise in satyagraha against Hitler, thus indicating his belief in the possibility of satyagraha against an oppressive national government in Europe;[15] and he appealed to the victims of German and Japanese imperialism to lay down their arms and resist the aggressors nonviolently. While he appealed to Germany and Japan to give up the method of arms and embrace the method of the "soul force," he also appealed to the Czechs, Poles, Norwegians, French, English and Chinese to resist German and Japanese aggression through national satyagraha.[16] He also advised the Indian people not only to desist from supporting the British war effort, but to prepare for nonviolent defence against a potential Japanese or German invasion.[17] Some of the methods suggested by him for such national satyagraha against foreign aggression as a substitute for war, which we shall discuss presently, indicate that he may have regarded the largeness of territory and population as an advantage in such satyagraha. But he never in fact suggested, as did Mao in the early part of his career, that resistance by a small state with a small population and urban structure would in fact be unsuccessful.

Even nuclear weapons, both Mao and Gandhi have thought, would not make any difference to the validity of people's war and satyagraha respectively. Before the invention of nuclear weapons Mao argued, as we have seen, that the masses of people rather than military technology were the deciding factor in all warfare. Even after the first atom bomb had been used, he failed to see any reason for changing this thesis. As he told Anna Louis Strong in 1946: "The atom bomb is a paper tiger used by the US reactionaries to scare people. It looks terrible, but in fact it isn't. Of course the atom bomb is a weapon of mass slaughter, but the outcome of a war is decided by the people, not by one or two new types of weapon."[18] Since then the Chinese leaders have held fast to the view that the vast technological transformation of warfare in the nuclear age need have no mutational effect on the character of international relations, and people's wars can be fought all over the world, not only nationally but also internationally, on an even greater scale than before. The theoretical position on the subject is the old one enunciated by Mao. Lin Piao gave vivid expression to it, in the context of the massive development of nuclear weapons by the big powers, when he said: "However highly developed modern weapons and technical equipment may be and however complicated the methods of modern warfare, in the final analysis the outcome of a war will be decided by the sustained fighting of the ground forces, by the fighting at close quarters on battlefields, by the political consciousness of the men, by their courage and spirit of sacrifice.... The spiritual atom bomb which the revolutionary people possess is a far more powerful and useful weapon than the physical atom bomb."[19] Behind such theoretical generalization, however, lies a hard pragmatic calculation, namely, the improbability of a nuclear war actually taking place on account of the balance of terror. Lin Piao argued in 1966 that nuclear weapons could not be lightly used, since no country had a monopoly of them, and each nuclear power would be deterred by the fear of retaliation. Therefore, the fear of people's war escalating into nuclear war, as expressed by the Soviet Union, was an unreal one. This is proved by empirical evidence. "The Khrushchev revisionists maintain," said Lin Piao, "that a single spark in any part of the globe may touch off a world nuclear conflagration and bring destruction to mankind. If this were true, our planet would have been destroyed time and again. There have been wars of national liberation throughout the twenty years since World War II. But has any single of them developed into a world war?"[20] However, even if a nuclear war does break out, Mao and the other Chinese leaders are not afraid of it, because they are willing to accept the physical extermination of at least half of the human race in such a war for the sake of socialism, which they believe would inevitably triumph after the war. This line of reasoning was advanced by Mao in 1957 when he explained his own assessment of the consequences of a nuclear war in the following words:

> Out of the world's population of 2700 million, one-third—or putting the figure a bit higher, half—may be lost.... I debated this question with a foreign statesman. He believed that if an atomic war was fought, the whole of mankind might be annihilated. I said that if the worst came to the worst and half of mankind died, the other half would remain while imperialism would be razed to the ground and the whole world would become socialist. In a certain number of years there would be 2700 million people again and definitely more.[21]

Thus people's war can go on, according to Mao, in the first place because it is unlikely to lead to nuclear war on account of the balance of nuclear terror, and secondly because even if a nuclear war breaks out, there would still be enough people left to defeat the enemy through people's war and establish socialism all over the world. In this situation, to regard nuclear weapons as decisive in an international military confrontation, as not only the Western powers but also the Soviet Union do, is, according to Lin Piao, "to demoralize and spiritually disarm revolutionary people everywhere."[22]

Hence, according to Mao and the other Chinese leaders, there is no contradiction between their advocacy of people's war on a world-wide scale and China's strong commitment to a massive and long-range nuclear weapons programme. As they have persistently explained since the detonation of the first Chinese nuclear bomb in 1964, China's nuclear weapons programme is aimed at increasing the deterrent power of the socialist bloc vis-à-vis the USA and thus reducing the chances of a nuclear war further.[23] Perhaps they also wish to develop sufficient deterrent power of their own against all actual or potential nuclear enemies, including the Soviet Union. The Chinese nuclear deterrent, according to their calculations, would increase the chances of success for people's war everywhere by reducing those of a nuclear war. For the same reason, the revolutionary zeal of the Chinese people could not be allowed to wane, since the actual wars which they may have to fight would in all probability be only people's wars. This was perhaps the significance of Lin Piao's famous article on people's war, written a year after the first Chinese nuclear explosion, in which he not only urged the Chinese people to remain ever prepared for a people's war against the USA, but threatened the USA, interestingly enough, with people's war rather than with nuclear war.[24] It is equally interesting to note that neither in the first (1966) edition nor in the second (1967) edition of the *Quotations from Chairman Mao Tse-tung* is there any mention of China's nuclear power or programme.

Gandhi also remained unmoved in his faith in nonviolence by the development and use of nuclear weapons during the last three years of his life. The dropping of the atom bomb on Hiroshima, added to the experience of the Quit India Movement which had assumed a violent character and was quickly suppressed by the British Government, convinced him more profoundly than ever of the futility and immorality of all forms of violence, including violent resistance against foreign imperialism. At the end of 1945, while discussing the ineffectiveness of the Quit India Movement, he told his followers: "Today you have to reckon not with Britain alone, but the Big Three. You cannot successfully fight them with their own weapons. After all, you cannot go beyond the atom bomb. Unless we can have a new way of fighting imperialism of all brands, in the place of the outworn one of a violent rising, there is no hope for the oppressed races of the earth."[25] In the following year he repeatedly told the Indian people that the atom bomb had made violent resistance against imperialism obsolete from the purely utilitarian point of view, even if moral considerations were set aside.[26] Nonviolent resistance, he argued, was morally superior as well as more effective. In his own words:

> There has been cataclysmic changes in the world. Do I adhere still to my faith in truth and nonviolence? Has not the atom bomb exploded that faith? Not only has it not done so, but it has clearly demonstrated to me that the twins constitute the mightiest force in the world. Before it the atom bomb is of no effect. The two opposing forces are wholly different in kind, the one moral and spiritual, the other physical and material. The one is infinitely superior to the other, which by its very nature has an end. The force of spirit is ever progressive and endless. Its full expression makes it unconquerable in the world.[27]

He rejected the view held by many that Indian and other countries must have the experience of armed strength, including atom bombs, before gathering the courage to become nonviolent. Foreign imperialists, he argued, could not terrorize the Indians with atom bombs if the latter refused to be terrorized, just as they could not establish their superiority if the Indian people refused to consider themselves inferior. "We often make the mistake of thinking," he observed, "that we must first have things, before we cease to covet them. This tempting argument leads to the prolongation of the agony. Must I do all the evil I can, before I learn to shun it? Is it not enough to know the evil to shun it? If not, we should be sincere enough to admit that we love evil too well to give it up."[28] To American friends who argued that the atom bomb would eventually bring forth nonviolence among nations, Gandhi's answer was as follows:

> It has been suggested by American friends that the atom bomb will bring in *ahimsa*, as nothing else can. It will, if it is meant that its destructive power will so disgust the world, that it will turn away from violence for the time being. And this is very like a man glutting himself with the dainties to the point of nausea, and turning

away from them only to return with redoubled zeal after the effect of nausea is well over. Precisely in the same manner will the world return to violence with renewed zeal, after the effect of disgust is worn out.... The moral to be legitimately drawn from the supreme strategy of the atom bomb is that it will not be destroyed by counter bombs, even as violence cannot be by counter violence. Mankind has to get out of violence only through nonviolence.[29]

Hence, declared Gandhi, the atom bomb had not antiquated non-violence. "On the contrary, nonviolence is the only thing that is now left in the field. It is the only thing that the atom bomb cannot destroy."[30]

Finally, both Mao and Gandhi argue that people's war and satya-graha are weapons of the oppressed alone and cannot be applied in reverse. According to Mao, people's war can be used only by the op-pressed and revolutionary masses and not by imperialists, exploiters and counter-revolutionaries. He told Edgar Snow in 1965, when the latter referred to the study of Mao's military writings by Western military commanders, that the ideas propounded in his writings "would not work in reverse. They could be adapted only to the wag-ing of people's wars of liberation and were rather useless in an anti-people's war. They did not save the French from defeat in Algeria. Chiang Kaishek had also studied the Communist materials, but he had not been saved either."[31] Gandhi similarly argued that nonviolent methods would not succeed in defeating what was earlier secured through violence. It could be the weapon only of the oppressed and not of the oppressor. It could not be successfully used by the rich against the poor or by tyrants against the people for preserving their wealth or power obtained through direct or indirect violence.[32]

Needless to say, however, these numerous formal similarities be-tween people's war and satyagraha are overshadowed by the dia-metrically opposite accents laid by Mao and Gandhi on violence and nonviolence respectively, which make the operational contents of people's war and satyagraha mutually contradictory and their empiri-cal consequences radically different. The fundamental strategy of people's war, as developed by Mao during his long revolutionary ex-perience, through the five encirclement campaigns of Chiang Kaishek, the Long March, the Sino-Japanese war and the final stage of the civil war against Chiang Kaishek, is that of destroying the effective strength of the enemy, instead of holding territory, and preserving the strength of the people's armies. This means, operationally, abandoning positional warfare and adopting a combination of mobile and guerilla warfare. As Mao has repeatedly pointed out, the distinction between guerilla war and mobile war is one of degree and not of kind. Both are intended to harass, exhaust and annihilate the enemy and to avoid combat except when victory is certain. But guerilla war is of basic strategic significance for people's war, because "if they are to defeat a formidable enemy, revolutionary armed forces should not fight with a reckless disregard for the consequences when there is a great disparity between their own strength and the enemy's. If they do, they will suffer serious losses and bring heavy setbacks to the revolution. Guerilla warfare is the only way to mobilize and apply the whole strength of the people against the enemy, the only way to expand our forces in the course of the war, deplete and weaken the enemy, gradually change the balance of forces between the enemy and ourselves, switch from guerilla to mobile warfare, and finally defeat the enemy."[33] The basic tactics of guerilla war are: "The enemy advances, we retreat; the enemy camps, we harass; the enemy tires, we attack; the enemy retreats, we pursue."[34]

The object of both mobile and guerilla warfare, however, is to annihilate the enemy. "War of annihilation," as Lin Piao explained, "is the fundamental guiding principle of our military operations. This guiding principle should be put into effect regardless of whether mobile or guerilla warfare is the primary form of fighting."[35] It is, moreover, a fundamental principle of people's war to concentrate an absolutely superior force to annihilate the enemy forces one by one. In the words of Mao:

In every battle, concentrate an absolutely superior force (two, three, four and sometimes even five or six times the enemy's strength), encircle the enemy forces completely, strive to wipe them out thoroughly and do not let any escape from the net. In special circumstances, use the method of dealing crushing blows to the enemy, that is, concentrate all our strength to make a frontal attack and also to attack one or both of his flanks, with the aim of wiping out one part and routing another so that our army can swiftly move its troops to smash other enemy forces. Strive to avoid battles of attrition in which we lose more than we gain or only break even. In this way, although we are inferior as a whole (in terms of numbers), we are absolutely superior in every part and every specific campaign, and this insures victory in the campaign. As time goes on, we shall become superior as a whole and eventually wipe out all the enemy.[36]

But in order to annihilate the enemy, it is necessary to lure him deep into the territory of the invaded country, and for this purpose, to abandon some towns and districts before the advancing enemy deliberately in a planned way. For as Lin Piao explained: "It is only after letting the enemy in that the people can take part in the war in various ways and that the power of people's war can be fully exerted."[37] Luring the enemy deep is, therefore, an inalienable strategy of people's war.

There are many other strategic and tactical problems relating to the use of initiative, flexibility and planning in conducting offensives within the defensive; battles of quick decision within a protracted war; exterior lines operations within interior lines operations; coordination of guerilla warfare with regular warfare; the selection and establishment of base areas; strategic defensive and strategic offensive; the development of guerilla warfare into mobile warfare; and correct relationship of command. Mao has dealt with the complexities and solutions of each of these problems in great detail, in the light of the actual experience of people's war in China, and made it a military science of major international significance.[38]

The essential strategy of satyagraha, on the other hand, is that of nonviolent noncooperation, which in turn may lead to many different tactics, depending on the nature and circumstances of the struggle, from individual fasting to general strikes, violation of laws and the setting up of a parallel government, always subject to the minimum condition that the opponent must remain physically unharmed and even treated as a person with a wide charity, and that all the physical suffering, including the violence of the opponent, involved in the struggle must be borne by the satyagrahis themselves without retaliation.[39] So far as mass satyagraha against the government is concerned, Gandhi's argument is that the machinery of the government is sustained by the cooperation of the people. If that cooperation is withdrawn, the government logically ceases to govern. Carried to the extreme, he argued, mass noncooperation could paralyse any government and bring it to a standstill.[40] Applying this general principle of mass noncooperation to the concrete Indian situation in 1920, Gandhi observed:

> It is as amazing as it is humiliating that less than one hundred thousand white men should be able to rule three hundred and fifty million Indians. They do so somewhat undoubtedly by force, but more by securing our cooperation in a thousand ways and making us more and more helpless and dependent on them as time goes forward.... The British cannot rule us by force. And so they resort to all means, honourable and dishonourable, in order to retain their hold on India. They want India's billions and they want India's manpower for their imperialistic greed. If we refuse to supply them with men and money, we achieve our goal, namely, swaraj, equality, manliness.[41]

The initial programme of the Noncooperation Movement consisted of the surrender of titles and honorary offices; refusal to attend government levies, durbars or other government or semi-government functions; resignation of nominated posts in local bodies; withdrawal of children from schools and colleges run, aided or controlled by the government and the establishment of national schools and colleges on a private and voluntary basis; boycott of British courts by lawyers and litigants and establishment of parallel courts by the people for the settlement of disputes; refusal on the part of the military, clerical and labouring classes to offer themselves as recruits for service in Mesopotamia; withdrawal by candidates from elections to the reformed councils; boycott of foreign goods and the manufacture of cloth and other essential consumer goods through the development of village and cottage industries on the basis of a constructive programme. But very soon the movement crystallized into a threefold boycott, namely, the boycott of government-controlled schools and colleges, boycott of law courts and legislative councils, and boycott of foreign goods or *swadeshi*; and the building of parallel institutions and village industries. "If we can but free ourselves from the three-fold *maya* [snare, bondage, illusion] of the government-controlled schools, government law courts and the legislative councils," said Gandhi, "and truly control our education, regulate our disputes and be indifferent to their legislation, we are ready to govern ourselves...."

The last though not the least important part of the *maya* is *swadeshi*.
... If we would get rid of the economic slavery, we must manufacture
our own cloth, and at the present moment only by hand-spinning and
hand-weaving."[42]

Even civil disobedience, which involves the wilful violation of laws
considered unjust, is in practice only a variation of the strategy of
noncooperation, for refusal to obey laws is the most radical form of
noncooperation with the government. As Gandhi himself explained:
"A little reflection will show that civil disobedience is a necessary part
of noncooperation. You assist an administration most effectively by
obeying its orders and decrees. An evil administration never deserves
such allegiance.... Disobedience of the laws of an evil state is, therefore, a duty."[43] The nationwide nonviolent Civil Disobedience Movement was triggered off by the famous 241-mile Salt March by Gandhi
and his trained band of 78 followers from the Sabarmati Ashram to
the Dandi beach for violating the Salt Act (which had made salt
manufacture a government monopoly) in 1930, four years before
Mao made his bloody Long March of 2,000 miles from Kiangsi to
Yennan. The violation of the Salt Act which immediately spread like
a prairie fire, as Nehru said, was in fact a massive expression of noncooperation with the government by the people. Moreover, the Civil
Disobedience Movement also included such tactics as boycott of
British banks, insurance companies and other similar institutions,
just as the earlier Noncooperation Movement had been marked by
such forms of civil disobedience as non-payment of taxes in certain
areas.

A somewhat modified version of the same strategy was advocated
by Gandhi for resisting foreign aggression through satyagraha. He
was opposed to the Second World War because he believed that the
violence of the Allies was not the real answer to the violence of the
Nazis. The Allies, he argued, could win the war only by being
more violent than Germany. The net result, he argued, would
be an unprecedented increase in total violence. Nazism would be
defeated by an essentially superior Nazism, by whatever name it
might be called. Besides, "no cause, however just," argued Gandhi,
"can warrant the indiscriminate slaughter that is going on minute by
minute. I suggest that a cause that demands the inhumanities that
are being perpetrated today cannot be called just."[44] He, therefore,
suggested national satyagraha as the correct answer to German and

Japanese imperialism. The first stage of satyagraha for national defence, as suggested by him, would be a human wall at the frontier, which would invite the aggressive armies to march over the unarmed multitude with their guns, tanks and armoured cars. "The underlying belief in this philosophy of defence," he said, "is that even a modern Nero is not devoid of a heart. The spectacle—never seen before by him or his soldiers—of endless rows of men and women simply dying, without violent protest, must ultimately affect him. If it does not affect Nero himself, it will affect his soldiers. Men can slaughter one another for years in the heat of battle, for there it seems to be a case of kill or be killed. But if there is no danger of being killed yourself by those you slay, you cannot go on killing defenceless and unprotesting people endlessly. You must put down your gun in self-disgust." In his opinion, "an army that dares to pass over the corpses of innocent men and women would not be able to repeat that experiment." Therefore, said Gandhi: "I have no doubt in my mind that even a patched-up nonviolent army would take the wind out of Hitler's sails. I need not have his aeroplanes, his tanks, etc. He need not destroy our houses. Our nonviolent army would welcome him, and it may be that he would not dare to come."[45]

But supposing that the invading armies are not deterred by such a human wall and occupy the country anyway. Gandhi's answer would then be nonviolent noncooperation including civil disobedience. The entire population would refuse to work for the invaders, to help them in any way, to accept their currency, and even to give them water, "for it is no part of their duty to help anyone to steal their country."[46] The invaders, equipped with modern armaments, said Gandhi, might laugh at the idea of such noncooperation. "But India is a land of millions, and if they stand idle, the whole country stands idle. Nothing can be done with it; it is worthless. Civil disobedience, the invader would soon find, is a very powerful weapon indeed."[47] Would the invading armies destroy the country in anger and disgust? "Even if Herr Hitler was so minded," observed Gandhi, "he could not devastate 700,000 nonviolent villages. He would himself become nonviolent in the process."[48] Gandhi believed that if this new technique of nonviolent defence was adopted by a nation, even the loss of life would not in fact be greater than that caused by violent defence. "Practically speaking," he observed, "there would probably be no greater loss of life than if forcible resistance were offered to the invader. How many men have been killed in Holland, Belgium and France? Hundreds of thousands? Would the invading armies have shot down hundreds of thousands of men in cold blood if they had simply stood passively before him? I do not think so."[49]

The basic strategy of nonviolent resistance was further explained by Gandhi in connection with a third dimension of satyagraha which is altogether missing from people's war, namely, satyagraha against socio-economic injustice, irrespective of the form of government. Gandhi did not regard all history as the history of class struggles, or all social contradictions as manifestations of a fundamental class contradiction. Nevertheless, he was profoundly conscious of the need for resolving labour-capital and landlord-peasant conflicts in India and elsewhere, and prescribed satyagraha rather than violent class struggle as the only effective means to it. But the strategic compulsions of the mass movements led by him in India, and earlier in South Africa, offered him very little opportunity to deal with the problem of class relations, as I have explained before. In South Africa he did organize a spectacular nonviolent strike of Indian miners, but it was more of a protest against the racialist policy of the South African Government than one pertaining to class relations. The first satyagraha organized by him in India in 1917 was against the economic and social injustices suffered by the indigo cultivators of the Champaran District of Bihar; but his civil disobedience on this occasion was against the British authorities rather than against the planters themselves, although the peasants actually benefited from the enquiry which the government ordered as a result of the satyagraha. The Kheda satyagraha of the following year, against the unwillingness of the Bombay Government to remit the land revenue of the peasants of the district in spite of a serious crop failure, involved civil disobedience on the part of the peasants in the form of nonpayment of land revenue, and did not involve the problem of class relations. The Bardoli satyagraha of 1928 against an exorbitant in-increase of land tax likewise involved civil disobedience in the form of nonpayment of taxes to the government, and noncooperation in the form of resignation of local offices and the setting up of a parallel local administration.

But in all these cases the essential elements of satyagraha as a means for the rectification of economic injustice were present. There was complete nonviolence and willingness to suffer the consequences of disobedience including imprisonment, confiscation of land and property, and physical violence. The same basic principles and tactics could be applied, argued Gandhi, for solving the problem of land-lord-peasant relations. As we have seen before, he was in principle against all exploitative forms of private property, and was a strong advocate of the ownership of all land by the tillers of the soil, and even of nationalization of land, if necessary. He advocated a system of trusteeship, consisting of voluntary self-abnegation on the part of the landlords and capitalists and acceptance of the peasants and labourers by them as co-partners of their wealth, but prescribed satyagraha by the exploited classes for enforcing their rights if the exploiting classes failed to see reason.

If the landlords refused to reduce themselves to poverty and to re-cognize the right of the peasants to the land cultivated by them, the latter must, according to Gandhi, resort to satyagraha in the form of nonviolent noncooperation, or in other words, nonviolent agricul-tural strikes. They would refuse to cultivate the land. If the landlord asked them to quit the land, they would do so, but at the same time tell the landlord in unmistakable terms that the land in fact belonged to them. Since it would be impossible for the landlord to till all his land personally, he would be compelled sooner or later, argued Gandhi, to agree to the conditions laid down by the peasants. Should the landlord attempt to replace the striking tenants by others, non-violent agitation should continue until the blacklegs saw their error and made common cause with the strikers.[50]

Basically the same method would apply to industrial strikes as well. Gandhi was personally instrumental in organizing and leading an industrial strike at Ahmedabad in 1918, which Erik H. Erikson con-siders to be an event of fundamental significance for his life and thought.[51] This nonviolent strike, which was organized to enforce the workers' demand for higher wages, and was morally buttressed by a fast on the part of Gandhi, contained most of the essentials of satya-graha, although the success of the satyagraha was mixed up with various personal factors. Gandhi argued subsequently that if the basic principles and tactics developed by him in South Africa and at Ahmedabad were applied rigorously, a nonviolent strike could be-come an irresistible weapon in the hands of labourers for enforcing their just demands.[52]

The basic argument advanced by Gandhi for the efficacy of a nonviolent strike is quite simple. "Labour is free of capital," he said, "and capital has to woo labour, and it would not matter in the slightest degree that capital has guns and even poison gas at its disposal. Capital would still be perfectly helpless if labour would assert its dignity by making good its 'No.' "[53] Hence, the labourers are in a position to become co-sharers of the industry immediately they realize their own strength.

Both during the Ahmedabad satyagraha and afterwards Gandhi insisted on the strict observance of certain principles, if an industrial strike was to be called satyagraha and achieve its objective. First of all, of course, the strikers must remain totally nonviolent in thought and action, and copy the courage of the soldier without copying his objectives and methods. Indeed, nonviolent strikes would require greater courage than that of a soldier. Non-strikers, if any, must also be covered by the principle of nonviolence. Secondly, striking workers must not depend on public charity, but earn their living during the strike through self-employment in spinning, handicrafts, etc. Thirdly, there should be practical unanimity among the labourers regarding the decision to go on strike. Fourthly, an unalterable minimum demand should be fixed before the strike is embarked upon, instead of the usual practice of bargaining with a high demand on the expectation of a compromise settlement. Fifthly, strikes organized for political purposes must be kept separate from those with a primarily economic objective. Sixthly, workers engaged in essential services like the police and scavengers must never go on strike, but find other honourable methods for the rectification of their grievances. Last but not the least, a nonviolent strike must be launched for the rectification of a genuine injustice, and not simply as a matter of expediency or as a convenient stick to beat the employers with. The only sure method of obviating the possibility of workers from other areas replacing the strikers, said Gandhi, was the political education of the workers; but he observed that nonviolent strikes might not be successful in cases where the supply of labour was so great that all the striking labourers could be replaced by others.[54]

Gandhi advocated, performed, led or inspired satyagrahas also against contradictions of a social nature, like communalism and untouchability. Such satyagrahas usually assumed the forms of fasting, defiance of violence and *dharna* (a form of sit-down strike). For example, he personally fasted in 1932 in protest against the Communal Award of Ramsay MacDonald, which sought to establish separate electorates for India's untouchables; and in January 1948, shortly before his assassination, against communal violence in India. Similarly, a notable example of satyagraha in the form of defiance of violence and standing *dharna* took place under his inspiration and advice at Vaikom, in the former princely state of Travancore in 1924, in which the untouchables successfully resisted the restriction placed by the upper castes on the former's right to use a road passing by a temple.

Thus while people's war is essentially the art of the organized destruction of other human beings representing the enemy, through relatively inferior weapons, satyagraha is that of confronting the opponent with a moral challenge and a socio-psychological situation. In spite of all the emphasis on the political mobilization and "spiritual power" of the masses, people's war is the function of an essentially military machine. The long-term strategy followed by Mao in China was that of a progressive increase of the military and technological power of the people's armed forces, and a combination of the maximum possible military power with the maximum possible revolutionary consciousness at every stage of the war. The adversary, whether it was a national government or a foreign power, had to be eventually defeated by armed force. Although people's war is an enveloping political war, it is, like all wars in their essence, politics plus war. Gandhi's strategy, on the other hand, was to rely solely on the revolutionary consciousness and organized will power of the people, and to face the opponent with an all-pervasive socio-political warfare which began with a deliberate farewell to arms and remained strictly nonviolent throughout. It was aimed at confronting the opponent with a military void which would render his superior armaments unusable and irrelevant, while at the same time undermining the foundations of his political, social and moral authority.

It is logically impossible to deny Gandhi's contention that satyagraha is the only means which can preserve and promote the values of liberty, equality and fraternity. Every act of satyagraha, irrespective of whether its specific objective is attained or not, does in fact promote the basic values through the technique itself. In the first place, satyagraha, unlike people's war or other forms of revolution, is based entirely on individual moral responsibility. In a revolution, especially of the Communist type, the individual believes that he is merely accelerating the process of history by annihilating the class or other enemies, not in his individual capacity, but as a member of a class or other group which is an agent of history. He does not, therefore, consider himself in any way personally responsible or guilty for the violent suppression or extermination of other human beings in the course of the revolution. In this way not only is he destroying the liberty and even life of other individuals, but also himself acting as the supposed agent of history rather than as a free individual with personal moral responsibility for his acts. A satyagrahi, on the other hand, is constantly training himself for assuming the profound moral responsibility of changing social relationships and institutions; and in doing so he is not only refusing to violate the liberty of his adversary but subjecting himself alone to all the suffering involved in the act of satyagraha. He is thus acting himself as a free agent with individual moral responsibility as well as allowing his adversary to act in a similar manner. Secondly, since the whole basis of satyagraha is the recognition of the relativity of values and the essential equality of all human beings, it preserves and promotes equality in a very real sense. The satyagrahi confronts his adversary fearlessly, to the extent of sacrificing his life in the confrontation, and looks him in the eye as an equal, not as inferior or superior. As Erik H. Erikson has said of the nature of Asian-European relations (as an extension of Indo-British relations) after the Civil Disobedience Movement: "Asia could now look Europe in the eye—not more, not less, not up to, not down on. Where man can and will do that, there, sooner or later, will be mutual recognition."[55] Finally, fraternity or a wider love is the very essence of satyagraha. Since the satyagrahi covets neither power nor dominance either for himself or for his party or class, but is interested solely in securing justice, and is constantly training himself not to bear any ill-will for the adversary, he is an embodiment of fraternity although he is determined to extinguish the system for which his opponent is responsible. And since the opponent is neither physically harmed nor psychologically humiliated, but is enveloped by the satyagrahi in a wider love in the form of self-suffering, he emerges from the confrontation more humanized than before. Indeed, fraternity is the first principle of satyagraha and all other considerations are secondary; for Gandhi had the rare genius to perceive, through the vicissitudes of history, the fundamental truth that fraternity is a precondition to human liberty and

5

equality, although the most difficult of all the values to realize.

Thus there is an inviolable logical connection between satyagraha as a means for resolving social contradictions and the ultimate values of liberty, equality and fraternity as an end. Even where satyagraha is unsuccessful in achieving its immediate objective, it does preserve and promote these values, as Gandhi claimed. Where it is successful in achieving the desired justice, these values are doubly promoted. Hence a man who does not desire to undermine the fundamental values in his attempt to transform society must not deviate from the nonviolent way of resolving social contradictions. In the words of Erikson: "He will not permit himself or others to use foul means with the illusory justification that their continuance 'for a little while longer' will end in a utopian future when the truth will at last become the universal means—whereupon the world will forever after be free for democracy, or free for communism, or free for the stateless society, or whatever. What is true now will, if not attended to, never be true again; and what is untrue will never, by any trick, become true later."[56]

Nor can the claim of universality made by Mao for people's war be substantiated on the basis of historical evidence. People's war as a technique for resolving what was considered to be antagonistic contradictions was developed by Mao in historically relative circumstances, and its success was due in large measure to the external and fortuitous circumstance of the Japanese invasion. Although the Red Army was fairly successful against Chiang Kaishek in the first four encirclement campaigns, it was badly trapped and rendered helpless in the fifth, and it is the Long March which saved what remained of the Red Army. Besides, the relative success of the Red Army during this period, the success of the Long March and its ability to consolidate its position in Yenan were all partly due to the Japanese invasion which kept Chiang's forces divided between two fronts during the crucial years. The period of collaboration between the Kuomintang and the Communist Party which followed enabled the latter not only to consolidate and strengthen its position in the north, but to seriously alter the balance of forces at the end of the war. Besides, being in power and yet politically, militarily and administratively weak, unable to resist the Japanese or to control the country as a whole, the Kuomintang was seriously weakened and alienated from the masses during the war. The complete economic dislocation, drastic fall in production and runaway inflation caused by the war were also greatly responsible for the fall of the Kuomintang. Moreover, the immobile positional warfare resorted to by the Kuomintang during the civil war has been regarded by many observers as an important cause of the final defeat of its forces. Finally, the long leadership of Mao, which was a vital factor in the success of people's war in China, became possible due to the circumstance that he personally survived the long years of war although many of his colleagues fell all around him, which must be regarded as an accident of history, unless one is to regard it as a Hegelian "cunning of history" aimed at fulfilling its own predestined purpose.

Nowhere in the history of the world has anything analogous to people's war been successful except in the event of an external threat. Such earlier examples of successful wars analogous to people's war as the American War of Independence, the Spanish resistance against Napoleon, the French resistance in the Franco-Prussian War, the Irish Rebellion of 1916, the Yugoslav resistance against Hitler, and to some extent the Soviet war against Hitler's Germany, were all cases of resistance against foreign invasion. Subsequently, not only did people's war succeed in China in the context of the Japanese invasion, but the relatively analogous wars in Algeria and Vietnam have also taken place in the context of a strong external threat. As a matter of fact, with or without people's war, a Communist Party has come to power anywhere in the world to this day only during or soon after an external war, beginning with the First World War and the Russian Revolution. On the other hand, attempts at organizing people's war on a purely domestic basis have been squarely defeated in such countries as Burma and India. Even in the presence of an imperialist foreign power, such attempts were defeated in Malaya in the early 'fifties. Finally, China's massive and long-term build-up of nuclear weapons and the arguments used to justify this policy indicate that Mao and the other Chinese leaders do not themselves consider it possible to safeguard their external security by means of people's war alone.

Satyagraha in essence has definitely a much wider, if not universal applicability, although it was developed by Gandhi in some specific forms in the given historical conditions in India. In the first place, people's war is only a weapon for overthrowing a particular form of government which is based on class exploitation and for establishing the rule of the Communist Party. It ceases to be an instrument for resisting the possible tyranny of the new party-state once it has come into existence. Theoretically, of course, there can be no such tyranny and no need for resistance, since the new state is supposed to re- present the people and the hitherto exploited classes. But the causes of social conflict and political tyranny are much wider than mere exploitation, as modern Social Science recognizes, and Mao's own criticisms of the Soviet system, his own theoretical innovations re- garding the dynamics of a socialist state, and the politics of the Cul- tural Revolution indicate that such tyranny is quite possible, even in Mao's own opinion. How would the people resist such tyranny, if the armed forces are under the control of the government as in the Soviet Union, and do not side with the popular forces as they did during the Cultural Revolution in China? There is no clear answer to this question in Marxism-Leninism and even in the much more pragmatic ideology of Mao who has admitted that such a possibility exists. His only answer lies in the mass line, but as I shall try to show in the next chapter, the mass line as it prevails in China has very serious limitations as a vehicle of political protest. Satyagraha, on the other hand, is an instrument for resisting the tyranny of the state as such, irrespective of the form of government, although it may not succeed against an extreme and ruthless dictatorship, as Jacques Maritain, Karl Jaspers and others have pointed out.[57] Secondly, while people's war can be used for fighting only the state or an external aggressor, satyagraha can be used also for resolving economic and social con- flicts, at a national or local level. While the direct focus of the mass satyagraha movements led by Gandhi in India was on the ending of British rule, he considered satyagraha to be a universal means for the resolution of all contradictions and the multi-dimensional transfor- mation of society; and there were numerous satyagrahas by Gandhi and his followers not only against local injustices with which the British Government was directly concerned, but also against political, economic and social injustices perpetrated by Indians over other Indians. Strikes and other trade union methods, which have been relatively successful in safeguarding the interests of workers in many countries, can be regarded as close approximations to satyagraha in so far as they are based on nonviolence and just demands. Gandhi's own limited experiments in this field as well as the experience of trade union movements in various countries provide adequate grounds for regarding satyagraha as a potentially efficacious method for resolving class and other contradictions. Even Gandhi's apparently utopian scheme of defence against external aggression through satyagraha is not altogether without practical potentiality. Relatively successful experiments have been carried out with pure or mixed forms of nonviolent resistance against aggression in various countries in different periods of history, including the Hungarian resistance against Austria during 1849-1867, the German resistance against the Franco-Belgian invasion of the Ruhr in 1923, and the Norwegian resistance against Germany during the Second World War, though generally when armed resistance has been either unsuccessful or considered hopeless.[58] True it is that the state, whose moral responsibility is different from that of the individual, cannot decide to abstain from armed resistance against foreign aggression if there is a reasonable chance of the resistance being effective, in the given state of international relations. But where armed resistance is either unsuccessful or hopeless, satyagraha can be a reasonably effective method for making permanent occupation extremely difficult if not impossible, and for making clear to the outside world the utterly immoral position of the occupying forces. It is for this reason that many serious thinkers, including Bertrand Russell, Sir Stephen King-Hall and B. H. Liddell Hart, have recommended experiments with, and at any rate a serious consideration of, various forms of nonviolent defence against foreign occupation, especially in the context of nuclear war.[59]

Finally, satyagraha is more universally applicable than people's war from the point of view of the immediate empirical consequences. If people's war succeeds, the most immediate consequence, apart from the vast destruction of life and property, is the seizure of the state by a strong military power. If it fails, the only immediate consequence is the destruction of life and property. But whether satyagraha succeeds or fails to achieve the immediate objective, it does not cause any loss of life and property. In either case it not only promotes the ultimate values but also adds to the moral power of those who participate in it. Not all satyagrahas led or inspired by Gandhi in India were equally successful in achieving their immediate objectives: some were almost wholly successful, some only partially successful and a few wholly unsuccessful.[60] But they all led to a cumulative addition to the moral and political power of the Indian national movement. For instance, the immediate effect of the Noncooperation

Movement, which was suspended by Gandhi midway in 1922, was summed up by Jawaharlal Nehru when he said: "It was this extraordinary stiffening-up of the masses that filled us with confidence. A demoralized, backward and broken-up people suddenly straightened their backs and lifted their heads and took part in disciplined, joint action on a countrywide scale.... We became victims to the curious illusion of all peoples and all nations that in some way they are a chosen race."[61] It was this awakened mass power which prompted the Government of Bombay Presidency to say that "Gandhi's was the most colossal experiment in world history."[62] Hence, there can be no harm and only some possible gain if satyagraha is experimented with in any part of the world for resolving any kind of contradiction.

Gandhi's contribution to the resolution of contradictions does not lie in offering a static, universal and permanent solution to all possible social contradictions. It lies in pointing out that nonviolence rather than counterviolence constitutes the true negation of the other negation represented by direct violence or the indirect violence involved in exploitation and other forms of injustice. As Erikson has rightly pointed out: "In a period when proud statesmen could speak of a 'war to end war'; when the super-policemen of Versailles could bathe in the glory of a peace that would make 'the world safe for democracy'; when the revolutionaries in Russia could entertain the belief that terror could initiate an eventual 'withering away of the State'—during the same period, one man in India confronted the world with the strong suggestion that a new political instrument, endowed with a new kind of religious fervour, may yet provide man with a choice."[63] This choice, moreover, as Erikson has argued, is consistent with the evolutionary experience of man and points the way to the future of conflict resolution both within and among the nations of the world.[64] And this is not as commonplace a conclusion as it may appear to some, for it indicates the direction in which not only our ideals but also our efforts must lie, and makes us conscious of the all-important fact that if we must deviate from this direction under pressure of circumstances, it would be a matter of shame and regret rather than of glory and rejoicing.

CHAPTER FOUR

MASS LINE AND CONSTRUCTIVE PROGRAMME

THAT THE PROLETARIAN revolution and the dictatorship of the proletariat would be based on the broad support and active participation of the masses is an old Marxist idea, but in the given socio-political context of China it struck deep roots in Mao's mind when he was quite young and not yet a convinced Marxist. During the May Fourth Movement he wrote an article on "The Great Union of the Popular Masses" which revealed a strong populist political outlook, derived probably more from the Chinese milieu than from Marxism. This populist and quasi-anarchistic urge to change the destiny of China through the organized effort of the masses of people rather than through legal and bureaucratic methods apparently became increasingly stronger with Mao's advancing age and growing political experience, and is regarded by him, as explained before, as the principal instrument for transforming the character of the state and society and the relationship between the two. The essence of the mass line was formulated by him in an essay on "Some Questions Concerning Methods of Leadership" in 1943 in terms of the Marxist theory of knowledge as follows:

In all the practical work of our Party, all correct leadership is necessarily 'from the masses, to the masses'. This means: take the ideas of the masses (scattered and unsystematic ideas) and concentrate them (through study turn them into concentrated and systematic ideas), then go to the masses and propagate and explain these ideas until the masses embrace them as their own, hold fast to them and translate them into action, and test the correctness of these ideas in such action. Then once again concentrate these ideas from the masses and once again go to the masses so that the ideas are preserved in [*sic*] and carried through. And so on, over and over again in an endless spiral, with the ideas becoming more correct, more vital and richer each time. Such is the Marxist theory of knowledge.[1]

Mao explained, in this and other writings, the detailed methods of forming a nucleus of party activists in every institution or locality, and rousing the less active masses through the initiative of this nucleus. He argued that a leadership which was divorced from the mass line could only be subjectivist and bureaucratic, and, therefore, detrimental to the radical transformation of social institutions in terms of popular urges and needs. The main principle of the mass line, as enunciated by Mao time and again, is that neither the re-volution nor the political, economic and cultural transformation of society can be successfully accomplished without the support and active participation of the masses, and that, on the other hand, any obstacle, however great, in any sphere of national development, can be definitely overcome if the invincible and indestructible power of the masses is mobilized by a correct application of the mass line. When the Communist Party is in opposition, the mass line, as we have seen, is primarily intended to broaden the base of people's war which, as Mao said, is a war of the masses and can be waged only by mobilizing the masses and relying on them. In the era of socialism, on the other hand, it is primarily intended to facilitate the all-round reconstruction of society. "The wealth of society," said Mao, "is created by the workers, the peasants and the working intellectuals. If only they take their destiny into their own hands, follow a Marxist-Leninist line, and energetically tackle problems instead of evading them, there is no difficulty in the world that they cannot resolve."[2] In any case, whether before the seizure of power or after, the masses constitute "the real iron bastion which it is impossible, and absolutely impossible for any force on earth to smash."[3]

Gandhi's idea of constructive work as one of the two principal instruments of social transformation springs from the recognition of the need for constructing the infrastructure of the just society gradually and over an indefinitely long period of time, as I have explained in Chapter II. The society representing the ultimate values, he argued, could not be built by any "short-violent-cuts to success," for, as he explained: "It will not drop from heaven all of a sudden one fine morning. But it has to be built up brick by brick by corporate

self-effort."[4] Such a constructive endeavour by the masses will itself
have a value-creating function at every step and hence lead to a progressive realization of values in the body social. Being based on the
bread-labour of large masses of men, the constructive programme
would be free from exploitation and other forms of violence and,
therefore, promote fraternity. Moreover, the programme would
gradually lead to the construction of a highly decentralized socio-
economic infrastructure which alone could be defended, thought
Gandhi, as we have seen, through nonviolence. Freedom, both individual and collective, is also ensured by the constructive programme,
because the individual and collective effort involved in it is voluntary
and creative in nature, and secondly because it would make the
masses and their institutions free from the control of the state or any
other superior authority. As a matter of fact, Gandhi insisted that
the wholesale fulfilment of the constructive programme was equi-
valent to the attainment of *poorna swaraj* or full freedom for society
as a whole.[5] Finally, since the constructive programme is free from
either the propensity or the opportunity for private accumulation
and exploitation, and is based on and conducive to love and cooperation, equality, in Gandhi's view, would also necessarily follow from
it.

Since satyagraha as visualized by Gandhi is a more fundamental
and perennial means of social transformation than people's war, the
logical and organizational link between the constructive programme
and satyagraha is also more fundamental and perennial than that
between people's war and the mass line. In the first place, the constructive programme constantly trains satyagrahis in value-laden social action. Being engaged in bread-labour, the moral discipline of
constructive work, and service to the people rather than to self, the
countless volunteers participating in the constructive programme
become increasingly qualified for the task of social transformation
through nonviolence and especially for the voluntary suffering inherent in satyagraha. Hence Gandhi stated categorically that the
constructive programme "is the basis of the training for the nonviolence of the brave."[6] Secondly, it provides the armies of satyagrahis with a minimum wherewithal and makes them independent of
both the government and the vested interests. They become self-
employed free agents who can court arrest and imprisonment whenever necessary. Thirdly, it provides the mass base to a satyagraha

movement, as does the mass line to people's war, by ensuring the active cooperation of the people. The masses of men and women, young and old, who are engaged directly or indirectly in the constructive work, are necessarily sympathetic to the cause and to the participants in the struggle, although most of them are not directly engaged in satyagraha. It is the mass base provided by the constructive programme which sustains the satyagrahis before, during and after a satyagraha movement. Fourthly, the constructive programme is an essential adjunct of noncooperation which is the basic strategy of satyagraha. Noncooperation, whether against a national government, a foreign power or domestic vested interests, is always against institutions and systems of injustice; and it can be successful only when the people are able to build alternative institutions and systems to suit their requirements. The building of such parallel institutions takes place through the constructive programme. Fifthly, since the programme involves the building of new and just social institutions which would naturally come into contradiction with existing vested interests and even with the state, it highlights focal points of injustice and hence also areas of potential satyagraha. Finally, it creates the social environment in which nonviolence and the other ultimate values progressively become a way of life.

Although Mao and Gandhi visualized the mass line and the constructive programme respectively as general instruments of social transformation, the actual application of these techniques in China and India took place in given historical conditions and had an inevitably specific character. But while the mass line developed in China pragmatically without any particular blueprint (though in terms of the preconceived ideological perspectives of Marxism-Leninism and Maoism), in India Gandhi at one stage (in 1941) presented an outline of a particular constructive programme relative to the given situation for the benefit of his workers. It contained nineteen items including the establishment of communal harmony, abolition of untouchability, voluntary prohibition, establishment of *khadi* (home-woven cloth made from home-spun yarn) production centres and other village industries in each village, introduction of a new or "basic" education, organization of "true political education of the adult by word of mouth," emancipation of women, village sanitation and hygiene, development of provincial languages and the abolition of English, establishment of economic equality, development of peasant, labour and student organizations on a non-political basis, uplift of the aboriginal tribes, service and rehabilitation of lepers, and improvement of cattle. As I have tried to show elsewhere, this was not a well-drafted document, and gives only a very rough and narrow idea of the broader programme of constructive work which had been taking place in India under Gandhi's leadership since 1922,[7] but it gives a reasonably clear idea of the kind of constructive work Gandhi had in mind for the multi-dimensional transformation of Indian society on a decentralized and voluntary basis. I shall concentrate here only on a broad comparison of the salient features of the mass line of Mao and the constructive programme of Gandhi from the point of view of economic, socio-cultural and political change.

Decentralized economic development, with the maximum possible utilization of manpower and local resources, was an imperative economic necessity imposed by the vast populations, absence of industrialization, shortage of capital, abysmal poverty and mass unemployment which constituted the economic background of social transformation in China and India in the first half of this century. This pattern of development still remains a necessity in large parts of Asia, especially in the populous countries, as Gunnar Myrdal has explained in detail.[8] Both Mao and Gandhi, who knew the real conditions of their own countries much better than the upper class intellectuals who dominated political thinking before them, recognized this economic imperative and sought to give it an effective organizational shape through the mass line and the constructive programme respectively. Within the given political framework of China, the mass line necessarily implied the activization of the masses by the Communist Party cadres for economic reconstruction, primarily at the village level, and to some extent also in the cities. The programme of land reforms, both before and after the Communist Party came to power, was carried out mainly by party activists who went in their thousands to the villages, aroused the peasant masses and organized them for the implementation of the reform programme. Subsequently, the multi-staged institutional reorganization of agriculture, from the mutual aid teams to the lower-stage cooperatives and higher-stage cooperatives or collective farms and finally to the communes, was organized and implemented by thousands of party cadres all over the countryside with the help of the ninety per cent of the peasantry with whom Mao asked his party cadres to unite in pursuit of the mass line.[9] The same story was repeated with regard to the development of small-scale industries, both in rural and urban areas. The declared objective of Mao in the pursuit of the mass line in the economic sphere was the eradication of the contradictions between the forces of production and the relations of production, between China's poverty and the goal of a strong and prosperous Chinese nation, between the towns and the villages, and between capitalism and socialism. But the most important of all the goals in the given situation was perhaps the generation of a larger volume of agricultural surplus through collectivization than would otherwise have been possible, as Mao himself explained at the time.[10]

The maximum utilization of the mass line for decentralized economic development took place during the Great Leap Forward Movement (which also coincided with the programme of communization) which was launched in 1957 ostensibly with a view to overtaking advanced capitalist countries like the UK within fifteen years. According to official reports from Peking, for example, between the winter of 1957 and April 1958, 100 million peasants had been sent to work on water conservancy projects, and they completed some 56,000 million cubic metres of earth and stone work by putting in 13,000 million workdays in three months.[11] The "battle of iron and steel," involving the collection of iron ore and coke from all possible sources and the manufacture of steel in backyard furnaces, also witnessed a spectacular mass mobilization in pursuit of the mass line. In the Lin-yi county of Shantung province more than 100,000 civilian workers were mobilized to transport iron ore and coke; and "queuing up into long lines day and night, many of them slept only three hours a day." In the Chinkiang mountain area of Hunan province, "no matter whether the person was an old man... or a child under ten, whether a worker, peasant, cadre or housewife, everybody took up a hammer and a basket and ran into the mountains; when it was dark there was light everywhere, and the sound of explosions continued throughout the night."[12] In areas of the northwest, peasants and workers engaged in steel production "fought round the clock, eating and sleeping beside the furnaces," and elsewhere they stuck to their posts in torrential rain or freezing temperatures.[13] In Kwantung province some 7 million peasants were rushed to the mountains to collect iron ore, from there back to their homes for autumn harvesting and preparing the land for the next crop, and then mobilized for work on irrigation and flood control projects.[14] Similar mass efforts were also made for the collection of compost and other organic manure. By mid-winter 1959 more than 70 million people or about 10 per cent of China's entire population were reported to be engaged in this work.[15] The setting up of urban communes and street industries also involved mass economic activity in the urban areas on a big scale. Transport and communication undertakings and even marketing organizations came under the impact of the mass line.

The failure of the Great Leap Forward to achieve the high economic objectives—the partial dislocation of the economic system and the fall in both agricultural and industrial production partly caused by it—is to be explained by the extreme haste with which the movement was organized and the scant attention paid to the technical aspects of agricultural and industrial production, irrigation, water conservancy, etc. and should not be interpreted as an argument against such mass mobilization for economic development in a populous agricultural society. On the contrary, the Great Leap represented a correct realization on the part of Mao Tse-tung that if dependence on external capital is to be minimized (as was necessary for China since the beginning of the Sino-Soviet conflict in 1956), an agricultural country trying to industrialize itself quickly must rely primarily on the mobilization of all available manpower and indigenous resources for decentralized agricultural and industrial development. The basic soundness of this policy was vindicated in the 'sixties when a modified form of mass mobilization, based on the avoidance of undue haste and technical feasibility, resulted in major gains in both industrial and agricultural production.

The particular constructive programme formulated by Gandhi was aimed, so far as its purely economic aspect was concerned, at alleviating the poverty and unemployment of the Indian masses. As he explained time and again, he was strongly in favour of the development of village and cottage industries, because the problem of the Indian people, as he understood it, was the generation of employment rather than the creation of extra leisure time, and to generate small incomes in the vast rural areas where practically none existed. The traditional Indian economy had been based on village industries and handicrafts, and the destruction of this economy through the import of foreign manufactures as well as deliberate government policy during British rule was regarded by Gandhi as the principal cause of the economic degeneration of India and the extreme poverty of the Indian masses. Therefore, although he was not against the development of heavy and large-scale industries within limits, he argued that for a long time to come, the means of livelihood for the vast majority of the Indian people could come only from agriculture and handicrafts. In other words, as far as the economic argument is concerned, he advocated the fullest possible utilization of manpower in a situation in which capital was extremely scarce, and would remain scarce for a long time to come. From the economic point of view, this was the significance of his advocacy of the spinning wheel as an instrument for the generation of employment and income. Even Nehru, who was an advocate of rapid industrialization, realized this hard reality of the Indian economic situation when he observed in 1939 that "even a simple machine based on ancient technique like an ordinary spinning wheel today produces something out of nothing because it is worked in the spare or wasted hours of the villager."[16] As regards the actual extent of mass participation in the constructive programme, no statistics are available for such participation, but all the evidence indicates that literally millions of people participated in it throughout the country, especially in the rural areas.

The main difference between the mass line and the constructive programme, from the purely economic point of view, arises out of the widely divergent long-term economic perspectives of Mao and Gandhi, as explained in Chapter II. The acceptance of the Marxist goal of an industrially developed and affluent society naturally impels Mao to regard the use of the mass line for economic decentralization as a matter of short-term tactics rather than of fundamental long-term policy. Rapid industrialization based on the development of heavy and large-scale industries within the shortest possible time being the accepted goal of Chinese economic development, cottage and small-scale industries run by "guerilla methods" may at best be a supplementary sector of the economy in the long run, but certainly not the predominant pattern of economic activity. The mechanization of agriculture is also an accepted national policy, and will not require much of mass activity in the long run. Whatever remains of the mass line in economic development in the long run will probably apply to the management of industrial and agricultural undertakings rather than to industrial and agricultural production. But since Gandhi's anarchist ideal was based on a low level of technology and material well-being, he regarded the constructive programme as a long-term and fundamental instrument of economic change. While the minimum necessary heavy industries should be "centralized and nationalized," he argued, "they will occupy the least part of the vast national activity which will mainly be in the villages."[17] The long-term economic programme which would follow from his economic perspective is not one of replacing the cottage industries gradually by more mechanized or large-scale industries, but the other way about. That is why he declared categorically in 1940: "If I can convert the country to my point of view, the social order of the future will be based on the *charkha* and all it implies."[18] His idea of decentralized economic development through the constructive programme was, therefore, very different not only from the formally similar Maoist effort in China based on the mass line, but also from the utilitarian arguments for such decentralization advanced by Myrdal and other economists.

There can be little doubt that the Maoist perspective of gearing the mass line to a long-term programme of industrial and technological advance is more consistent with the realization of the ultimate values of liberty, equality and fraternity than the Gandhian perspective of using the constructive programme to bring into existence a materially stagnant society. Gandhi's argument, as we have seen, is that industrialization necessarily promotes concentration of power, exploitation, inequality and conflict, and hence detracts from liberty, equality and fraternity. Although this argument may at first seem reasonable in the light of the experience of the industrialized countries, there is in fact no reason for assuming a necessary connection between industrialization and the loss of values. Anthropological evidence does not indicate that there is necessarily a larger doze of the ultimate values in the non-industrial societies than in the industrial ones. The great variation among the industrial countries in this respect also indicates that it is possible to conciliate the ultimate values in different degrees through social policy. In fact Gandhi's conviction that man can transform himself and his social environment through his moral effort runs counter to the argument that man will fall a victim to his own technological innovations. It is more consistent with the view, shared by Marxists and practically all varieties of socialist and liberal thinkers, that it is possible for innovative social technology to regulate and mitigate, if not altogether extinguish, the disvalue effects of machine technology.

Far from being antithetical to the general value system, industrial and technological progress would in fact seem to be a necessary precondition for liberty, equality and fraternity, unless one defines these ultimate values from that narrow subjective point of view which regards the life of the individual as a purely inward phenomenon unrelated to his social environment. By securing material betterment for man and thus freeing him progressively from the elemental struggle for existence, industrial and technological progress not only adds substance to the legal and political forms of liberty and equality, but also opens up before humanity altogether new dimensions of creative and aesthetic self-expression. Liberty which is based on the denial of material well-being and creative self-expression on the material plane, equality which amounts to an equal sharing of poverty, and the fraternity of human beings who spend their waking hours in the struggle for bread and create nothing but children, can at best be a rather incomplete and even repressed form of liberty, equality and fraternity. As a matter of fact, the extreme poverty of the vast agricultural populations of Asia unquestionably warrants rapid industrial and technological progress, especially in the international context of the vast and widening gap between their living standards and creative performance and those of the industrial nations.

Moreover, the development of science and technology which precedes and accompanies industrial progress leads to the growth of human knowledge and the eradication of ignorance and superstition, which itself is a great value-creating force in every society, especially in a tradition-bound agricultural society. Science may, of course, be made to serve the cause of political dogma, but there is no necessary connection between them, and the widespread growth of scientific education does in fact tend to erode the foundations of such political dogmas in the long run. In any case, values based on the knowledge provided by science are more truly and strongly founded than those based on ignorance.

Besides, the development of science, technology and industry, by progressively improving the means of transport and communication, creates conditions for collective material betterment and sharing of resources, dissemination of knowledge and social mobility, not only within the same society, but within human society as a whole. A

society in which the individual has the possibility of belonging in a
real sense to a wide human community would surely make liberty,
equality and fraternity more meaningful than one in which the absence of adequate means of transport and communication isolates
and alienates the individual or the small group from the rest of the
necessarily atomized human race.

Finally, rapid material betterment through technological and industrial advance is the dominant aspiration of the untold millions of
the economically backward areas of the globe, and a model of social
transformation which fails to accommodate this urge adequately is
bound to prove hopelessly unequal to the challenge of the times. This
is undoubtedly the most important reason why the pure Gandhian
model has rapidly lost ground even in India since independence, not
to speak of other Asian or African countries. This also explains why
the Maoist model of social transformation has such a wide appeal
among large sections of people in these countries.

Gandhi's broad anti-scientific and anti-technological bias, in spite
of his practical compromises is, therefore, on the whole a negative
contribution to the transformation of economically backward societies. But there is a positive, important and unquestionably valid element in his approach to science, technology and industrialization,
namely, that these are not ends in themselves, or even means for increasing national power as such; that these must be developed only
in order to promote certain ultimate values in the socio-political
system as a whole.

As regards socio-cultural change, the greatest similarity between
the mass line and the constructive programme lies in the sphere of
education. Before coming to power Mao had often emphasized the
need for proper education of the masses as well as of party and army
cadres. In his theoretical writings he had also developed the foundations of Marxist-Leninist education, the central point of which is
that education must be based on the dialectical materialist view of
history and hence a combination of theory and practice. In the context of China's mass illiteracy and economic backwardness, Mao
applied this theory to organize an educational system that is dove-
tailed into the production plans. In addition to universal primary
education, a national network of "spare-time" and "part-time"
educational institutions has been introduced throughout the country.
In the spare-time schools the factory workers and farmers are given

6

general and political education, while in the part-time institutions the students work on a part-time basis in fields and factories. As a result education has assumed a mass character never possessed by it before in Chinese history. Practically all the school-age children now receive some form of elementary education, and the bulk of the adult population has also been brought into the fold of the new educational system. Mass illiteracy, the traditional social curse of China, has been largely eliminated, the attempt in this direction being associated with a modification of the language. Simultaneously, great emphasis has been laid on the rapid expansion of scientific and technical education, in order to promote a scientific outlook among the masses as well as to catch up with and even overtake the technologically advanced nations in this respect. Another interesting and important educational trend introduced by Mao is the attempt to eliminate the distinction between intellectual and manual labour. This is to be achieved through the double process of education of workers and peasants and participation in productive labour on the part of the intellectuals. Mao has often criticized the domination of the Chinese educational institutions by "bourgeois intellectuals," and during the Great Leap Forward and the whole decade of the 'sixties there was a persistent campaign for the socialist transformation of the Chinese intelligentsia through "productive labour."[19]

Gandhi was not a materialist in any sense, and was not even familiar with intricacies of the Marxist theory of knowledge, and yet he argued like Mao that true knowledge and education could only result from participation in productive labour. He also emphasized like Mao the great importance of physical education without which, he believed, education became only a grotesque and lopsided affair; and true physical culture, he argued, could come only from productive labour. Another reason for Gandhi's emphasis on the participation of students in productive labour is that like Mao, he wanted the students and educational institutions to be linked to the productive process and to contribute to the national wealth. He expected the educational institutions to be self-sufficient, on the basis of the productive labour of the students, with regard to recurring expenses including salaries of teachers, though not in respect of land, buildings and other capital investments. The state was to purchase the produce of the schools and guarantee employment of the students in the crafts they had mastered. Moreover, as we have seen before, Gandhi considered bread-labour to be conducive to the moral development of man, and applied this principle also to education. Without productive labour there could be no moral and spiritual development of the student, and without such development education would prove to be a "poor, lopsided affair." Intellectual, physical, moral and spiritual training constitutes, according to Gandhi, an indivisible whole, and productive labour is, therefore, an integral part of true education. In the given conditions of India Gandhi regarded spinning as a good form of productive labour, especially for its organizational simplicity. He did not rule out other handicrafts, and his main emphasis was on productive labour and employment-oriented education. He also advocated, as we have already noted, adult education by word of mouth on a countrywide scale.

Another remarkable similarity between the educational ideas of Mao and Gandhi is that both of them advocated a reduction of the period of schooling so as to make education serve the practical needs of the people. Although Gandhi was not opposed to higher education as such, he was more or less indifferent to it, and considered a schooling of seven years to be sufficient for most people. Within these seven years, he believed, all that was being taught in India up to the Matriculation standard (except English) could not only be included but taught more effectively. The schools were to be generally co-educational. Such a production-oriented seven-year education of the masses Gandhi called "basic education" or *nayee talim* (new education). In it education would be centred round some handicraft, and even knowledge of other subjects like history, geography, mathematics and science would be imparted to the students through the medium of their craft training and productive labour. Moral instruction, consisting of "fundamental ethics" rather than denominational instruction, was to be a part of the syllabus (in Mao's educational system this is substituted by political indoctrination). If the members of any religious denomination wanted special denominational instruction for their children, they were to pay for it.[20]

Both Mao and Gandhi believed that when there was a great national cause involved, formal schooling was of relatively less importance. Gandhi gave a call to all students during the Noncooperation Movement to leave their schools and colleges and join the national movement, as Mao did in China on several occasions, especially during the Cultural Revolution. Many of Gandhi's close followers and the bulk of his vast army of constructive workers in fact came from volunteers who had given up their formal education to join the freedom movement led by him.

But while Mao expected his educational system to accelerate the process of social transformation through the heightened class and revolutionary consciousness of the younger generation as well as the growth of science and technology, Gandhi believed that the *nayee talim* of his conception would bring about a nonviolent and gradual transformation of social relations towards a low-technology anarchist society. In his own words:

> My plan. . . is thus conceived as the spearhead of a silent social re-volution fraught with the most far-reaching consequences. It will provide a healthy and moral basis of relationship between the city and the village and thus go a long way toward eradicating some of the worst evils of the present social insecurity and poisoned re-lationship between the classes. It will check the progressive decay of our villages and lay the foundation of a juster social order in which there is no unnatural division between the "haves" and the "have-nots" and everybody is assured of a living wage and the right to freedom. And all this would be accomplished without the horrors of a bloody class war or a colossal capital expenditure such as would be involved in the mechanization of a vast continent like India. Nor would it entail a helpless dependence on foreign im-ported machinery or technical skill. Lastly, by obviating the neces-sity for highly specialized talent, it would place the destiny of the masses, as it were, in their own hands.[21]

The attempt of both Mao and Gandhi to give a mass basis to education and to dovetail the educational system into the productive process were great contributions, from the purely utilitarian point of view, to the social transformation of China and India in the context of mass illiteracy, poverty and unemployment. Their common ad-vocacy of abolition of the distinction between intellectual and manual labour through participation in production is also of great signi-ficance for the two old societies in which manual work was tradi-tionally looked down upon, but which nevertheless required a mas-sive productive effort for economic betterment. But such utilitarian considerations were obviously not the basis of Gandhi's educational theory, for he wanted the new education advocated by him to be an instrument for bringing his own low-technology anarchist utopia into existence, rather than as a utilitarian device for the development and employment of human resources in a historically given situation; and the utopia to which he would take us would not instantiate the ultimate values in their true form, as I have already argued. To be truly creative of the ultimate values, the Gandhian scheme of education must be integrated with science and technology to the maximum possible extent.

In view of their divergent attitudes to the transformation of social relationships, the approaches of Mao and Gandhi to the traditional and fundamental problem of social stratification in India and China were quite different. According to Mao, the class struggle is the only means for the levelling down of the stratified traditional society. While people's war is the highest form of this class struggle and the primary instrument for the radical alteration of social relations, even in the era of socialism the class struggle continues, though at a non-antagonistic level, for ending the legacy of the class society. While it continues on the one hand through institutional reorganization like collectivization, communization and nationalization, it also takes the form of various mass campaigns aimed against the remnants of the former exploiting classes. Through this double process operating under Mao's personal guidance, the class character of traditional Chinese society has largely been obliterated. In February 1957 Mao stated that although the main socialist transformation of China had already been completed, the remnants of the old classes still existed and a long period of further class struggle would be necessary to eliminate them.[22] But he also stated one year later that "the former exploiting classes are reduced to mere drops in the ocean."[23] The Great Leap Forward and the Cultural Revolution seem to have further undermined the position of the remnants of the old classes. The major and minor warlords who used to dominate the Chinese people politically as well as socially have been eliminated as a class. At the next lower level, the landlord-gentry class has also been virtually wiped out from the Chinese social scene. Although Mao's attempt to abolish all distinctions among the peasantry through the rural communes has not so far succeeded, the rich peasants have disappeared as a class. The relatively small industrial and merchant-capitalist class of pre-Communist China has been almost entirely absorbed in the new state-controlled economic system. The Chinese intelligentsia, which had assumed a revolutionary role since the early part of this century, has been ideologically and politically transformed to a considerable extent, although if the Hundred Flowers Movement and its aftermath and the Cultural Revolution are any guide, the ideological transformation of the intelligentsia is still far from complete.

The social stratification of Gandhi's India, as I have pointed out in Chapter I, was much more complex than that of China, and there were many dimensions to it like untouchability, communalism and caste which were absent from the Chinese social milieu. Gandhi's task in applying the constructive programme and satyagraha to the problem of social stratification was, therefore, much more difficult than that of Mao. Added to this was Gandhi's dedication to non-violence, and its operational consequence, namely, a quasi-religious, gradualist and adaptive approach to social transformation. It is, therefore, not surprising that the constructive programme included only two elements of social stratification, namely, untouchability and communalism, and neither caste nor class.

So far as untouchability and its attendant strictures are concerned, Gandhi declared them to be "immoral" and urged their complete eradication. In fact, if there is any one single social evil against which Gandhi fought persistently throughout his career, it is untouchability. He declared time and again that untouchability militated against all the ultimate values cherished by him, and that freedom from foreign rule would be meaningless if such social injustices were present in independent India. Hindu society in particular, he argued, would disintegrate if untouchability was not abolished immediately. During his fight for the right of the untouchables to enter Hindu temples and his general work for the abolition of untouchability, he often had to face strong opposition from the orthodox Hindu community. He undertook in 1932 a "fast unto death" against the Communal Award of Ramsay MacDonald, which proposed separate electorates for the untouchables. He started publishing the weekly journal *Harijan* (children of God) in the following year and continued to use it as an organ for his struggle against untouchability till the end of his life. The important place assigned to it in the constructive programme, and the numerous satyagrahas organized all over India under his general guidance for ending this social evil also indicate that he tried to give the anti-untouchability campaign the character of a mass movement as far as possible within the strategic compulsions of the freedom movement.

But unlike many other educated Indians, including Dr B. R. Ambedkar, the leader of the untouchables, Gandhi believed that there was no inseparable connection between caste and untouchability. In fact, in many ways, he argued, caste was superior to the institution of class which had developed in Europe. Caste was not based on the "disruptive force" of distinctions of wealth as class was; it was merely an extension of the spirit of the family. In his opinion, social change takes place very slowly, and the institution of caste had recognized this fact by permitting new groupings. The social changes permitted by the caste system, he argued, were "quiet and easy as a change in the shape of the clouds." Therefore, even if the importance of environment as against heredity was recognized, the environment could be "conserved and developed" more through caste than through class.[24]

Gandhi observed that castes had performed a historically useful role in Indian society. They had prevented pauperism; acted as an institution of self-government and as a bulwark against oppression by the rulers; answered the religious as well as political needs of the people; and provided a vast experiment in social adjustment in the laboratory of Indian society.[25] But he wanted to reduce the thousands of castes and subcastes into the four basic *varnas* or hereditary social orders of the Hindu tradition. The law of *varna*, he declared, "is not a human invention, but an immutable law of nature—the statement of a tendency that is ever present and at work like Newton's law of gravitation. Just as the law of gravitation existed before it was discovered, so did the law of *varna*. It was given to the Hindus to discover that law."[26] He was opposed to the caste system only because it had unnecessarily multiplied the number of social divisions. "The division, however, into innumerable castes," he said, "is an unwarranted liberty taken with the doctrine [of *varna*]. The four divisions are all-sufficing."[27] He insisted, however, that *varna* represented a mere functional division and did not, in its pure form, involve a hierarchical social gradation. All functions had equal importance for society, and there ought to be no sense of high or low in this respect. For that very reason he was a strong advocate of the principle of hereditary occupations which lies at the basis of *varna*. In his opinion,

Abraham Lincoln should have been a woodchopper by profession like his father, and the President of the USA at the same time in an honorary capacity.[28]

Rejecting the position of those who argued that in order to abolish untouchability it would be necessary to abolish the entire caste system, including the four-fold *varna*, Gandhi observed that it was exactly the other way about. "The moment untouchability goes," he argued, "the caste system itself will be purified, that is to say, according to my dream, it will resolve itself into the true *varna dharma*, the four divisions of society, each complementary to the other and none inferior or superior to any other, each as necessary for the whole body of Hinduism as any other."[29] But he did not spell out how such a radical structural change in Indian society would come about with the eradication of untouchability, or where the untouchables, who were traditionally regarded as being outside the four orders, were to be accommodated if the *varna* system was to remain intact.

Gandhi was not the originator of the movement against caste and untouchability in India. Such ancient religions as Jainism and Buddhism developed in part as a protest against caste. The Bhakti or devotional movement of the middle ages in India was primarily an attempt at eradicating caste and untouchability. The various reformist movements of the nineteenth century were unanimous in rejecting caste and untouchability. Compared with such earlier movements, not to speak of the Marxist-Maoist approach to such problems, the views of Gandhi on caste and untouchability cannot be considered particularly radical, even after the situational compulsions have been taken into account.

As regards the problem of communalism, Gandhi said that he had become aware of it and dreamt of communal harmony at the age of twelve. All his life, especially in the last phase of his political career, he waged a relentless battle against the communal discord between Hindus and Muslims in India, and was finally assassinated by a fanatical Hindu for his "undue" sympathy for the Muslims and his "partiality" towards Pakistan. But the long series of Hindu-Muslim riots during the freedom movement, the demand by the large majority of Indian Muslims for a separate state, the mass communal killings on the eve of independence, the partition of the subcontinent, and finally the further large-scale communal disturbances in both the dominions and the migration of millions of people both ways on the

basis of their religion, offered indisputable evidence of the fact that
Gandhi's attempts at establishing communal harmony on the subcontinent had ended in failure. In fact Gandhi himself admitted his
failure on this front at the end of 1946,[30] and two weeks before his
martyrdom he pathetically exclaimed that he would "jump in the
evening of my life like a child to feel that the dream has been realized
in this life."[31]

At least part of the explanation for this failure can be found in
Gandhi's approach to the communal problem and its solution. At no
stage did he go into the deep-seated historical, economic, political
and cultural causes of communalism on the subcontinent, and regarded it as an artificial creation of the British Government. Sometimes he also attributed it to urban civilization and modern education. But he viewed the communal question as primarily a religious
one and believed that it would disappear if people gave up the idea of
the inequality of religions and learnt to respect religions other than
their own. This, in turn, he thought, would be possible if everyone
lived truly according to the teachings of his own religion.[32] In other
words, Gandhi adopted an ahistorical and simplistic approach to a
complex social contradiction. Only an elementary knowledge of
Indian history and sociology is necessary to realize that the solution
of the communal problem in India required a completely secular and
multi-pronged offensive, involving the attempt to achieve economic,
political and cultural integration of the two principal religious com-
munities. In fact, there is some justification for the opinion of those
who say that Gandhi's emphasis on religion aggravated rather than
eased the communal problem in India.

From the purely socio-cultural point of view, therefore, the Maoist
method of using the mass line for the nearly complete abolition of all
hierarchical social distinctions is more conducive than the constructive programme of Gandhi to equality and fraternity, and at least to
the extent that the abolition of the social hierarchy gives dignity and
self-confidence to the majority of people, also to liberty. Mao's attempt to replace religion by science as the basis of human relations is
also definitely more creative of the ultimate values than Gandhi's
endeavour to maintain mere harmony in communal relations on the
basis of equal tolerance of all religious dogmas. Gandhi's failure
to suggest any practical steps for abolishing the caste system is a
negative contribution to the ideal of human equality which he es-

poused in theory. For the same reason his advocacy of the abolition of untouchability must be viewed as a quasi-religious and half-hearted one, since it is impossible to see how the social status of the untouchables could have been raised without challenging the entire basis of the caste system. Even if the thousands of castes and subcastes could be reduced to the four basic orders or *varnas*, the untouchables would have always remained the fifth order or the *panchamas*, as they were designated by the ancient Hindu law-givers. Gandhi's nostalgic espousal of a hereditary division of society into four occupational *varnas* is detrimental to liberty, equality and fraternity alike, as well as to social mobility which is vital to the transformation of a traditional society. Nor can the entire approach of Gandhi to socio-cultural change be explained in terms of the religious tradition of the Indian people as opposed to the atheistic Chinese tradition or the strategic necessity for maintaining national unity in the struggle against British imperialism. For he even failed to offer any radical prescriptions which could be implemented in a different political situation, as he in fact did in the case of peasant-landlord and labour-capital relations.

But to compare the economic and socio-cultural aspects of the mass line and the constructive programme outside the framework of political change visualized by Mao and Gandhi respectively is not only to present a lopsided picture of the patterns of social transformation advocated by the two thinkers, but also to ignore the fundamental role of the political system itself in determining the character of economic and socio-cultural change; for political change by its very nature encompasses and moulds other social changes. And it is with regard to the basic political framework of social transformation that it is extremely difficult to defend Mao against Gandhi from the point of view of the ultimate values, although the Gandhian political model is also not above serious criticism.

In spite of his populist and anarchistic proclivities, Mao has applied to China the most fundamental political characteristic of Leninism, namely, the monopoly of political power enjoyed by the Communist Party. Neither the "democratic" revolution nor the socialist revolution in China, he wrote in 1939, could be accomplished "without a bolshevized Communist Party which is national in scale and has a broad mass character, a party fully consolidated ideologically, politically and organizationally."[33] He observed further in 1945 that "without the efforts of the Chinese Communist Party, without the Chinese Communists as the mainstay of the Chinese people, China can never achieve independence and liberation, or industrialization and the modernization of agriculture."[34] To him it was clear, therefore, as he declared in 1957, that "the Chinese Communist Party is the core of the leadership of the Chinese people."[35] Thus the mass line, though characterized by the organized constructive and agitational activity of the masses on a vast scale, is to be implemented by the Communist Party exercising a monopoly of political power and thus necessarily enforcing total control over the state as well as the society in a holistic sweep which leads to a Hegelian obliteration of the distinction between the two. Indeed, according to Mao's definition of "the people" and their "enemies," only those sections of the masses which implement the political and economic policies of the Communist Party belong to the category of people, while those who oppose these policies are the enemies of the people, irrespective of their class character or general socio-economic background. In his own words:

At the present stage, the period of building socialism, the classes, strata and social groups which favour, support and work for the cause of socialist construction all come within the category of the people, while the social forces and groups which resist the socialist revolution and are hostile to or sabotage socialist construction are all enemies of the people.[36]

It is important to realize further that the distinction between the Party and the army in Mao's China is one of degree rather than of kind. Almost from the beginning of his political career, he exhorted the members of the Communist Party to study military problems, to learn the use of arms and to take part in armed struggle. At the same time, the party members were also to participate actively in production and to become experts in problems of production. Since the middle 'thirties, when the Communists seized regional power, but especially after the victory of the Communist revolution, the cadres were also asked to be as adept in administration and management as in theory. Party men have always been expected, in other words, to be both red and expert. The functions of the army, as understood by Mao, are not different from those of the party. The army, of course, according to standard Marxist-Leninist principles, has always been expected to accept the control and ideological authority of the party. As Mao explained in 1938: "Our principle is that the party commands the gun, and the gun must never be allowed to command the party."[37] But the army is also expected to do considerable political, economic and educational work. As early as 1929 Mao observed that "The Chinese Red Army is an armed body for carrying out the political tasks of the revolution," and that "it should shoulder such important tasks as doing propaganda among the masses, organizing the masses, arming them, helping them to establish revolutionary political power and setting up party organizations."[38] He also repeatedly asked it to be not only a fighting force but also a production force.[39]

During the long period when Mao Tse-tung was in the opposition, there was practically no distinction between the party and the army. The leaders of the Communist Party were also the generals of the Red Army. The party cadres were political workers, producers and guerillas, all in one. After 1949, as the extent and importance of non-military functions increased rapidly in the new situation, an organizational distinction between the party and the army gradually developed, more or less resembling the Soviet system. But immediately before and after the Cultural Revolution the army took an active part in reorganizing the party along Maoist lines, and in the context of ideological divisions within the party, the army was urged to become "a great school of Mao Tse-tung's thought."[40] Lin Piao's nomination as the successor of Mao Tse-tung in the party Constitution also indicated the growing hegemony of the army over the party. The disgrace and violent death of Lin Piao and the fall of some other military leaders may indicate a reassertion by the party of its authority over the army. Yet, according to all available information, the army still rules the provinces, and in the context of universal military training and indoctrination, the distinction between the CCP and the PLA is far from clear. It is within the framework of total political control by this vast party-army complex that the mass line is required to operate. The entire mass line in China has been visualized by Mao in theory and practice as a programme of mass mobilization for achieving the political, economic and socio-cultural objectives of the party-army complex which has the monopoly of political power. The organization of the mass line rests on an inconceivably vast network of control units linking the small decision-making group in this party-army complex with the masses at the grass-roots. Every institution, whether it is a primary school, commune, factory or hospital, is controlled and administered by a small group of party activists who decide all the policies and programmes under directives from higher party echelons according to the so-called principle of "democratic centralism" under which, since the days of Lenin and certainly under Mao, centralism always prevails over democracy. There are students', youth, writers' and other professional associations and mass organizations which are nothing but levers of control in the hands of the party leadership. There are also general institutions like "neighbourhood committees" which are controlled by party activists and dominate every aspect of the lives of the entire population. And the whole process is finally controlled by a system of press, broadcasting and general communication monopolized by the state.

This vast control mechanism has been used in all possible ways to stabilize, strengthen and perpetuate the "people's democratic dictatorship." To begin with, it has been used to militarize and thus bring under the direct control of the party-army complex the entire population of China. During the Great Leap Forward an editorial in *Renmin Ribao* expressed the official policy in this respect when it said: "In the commune everyone should become a soldier. Young men eligible by age and all demobilized servicemen should be organized into militia, put under constant military training and required to shoulder the mission assigned by the state."[41] Since then production brigades divided into regiments, battalions, companies, platoons and squads have been organized for each commune and brought under direct control. Even in the "battle of iron and steel" and water conservancy projects the peasants and workers were organized in similar military formation. During the Cultural Revolution even education at all levels was taken over by the army under a directive from Mao which said:

The army should give military and political training in the universities, middle schools and the higher classes of primary schools, stage by stage and group by group. It should help in reopening school classes, strengthening organization, setting up the leading bodies on the principle of the "three-in one" combination and carrying out the task of "struggle-criticism-transformation"....

And the students should be persuaded to implement the teaching of Marx... and in military and political training they should not exclude those teachers and cadres who have made mistakes. Apart from the aged and the sick, these people should be allowed to take part so as to facilitate their remoulding. Provided all this is done conscientiously, it is not difficult to solve the problems.[42]

In spite of Lin Piao's fall and the relative stability of the last few years, the army's control over education does not seem to have been significantly reduced. All students, from the elementary to the university level, still receive compulsory military training. The Peking University, which before the Cultural Revolution had 10,000 general students on its rolls, was reported in February 1972 to have a militarized student force of only 2,600.[43] An attempt has also been made to use this enormous control system in the name of the mass line to indoctrinate the entire population in the ideology of the Chinese Communist Party and its chairman, on a scale which is without a shadow of doubt unparalleled in the history of the world. Every political, economic and social institution in China, big or small, particularly the entire educational system not excluding elementary schools, is a centre for compulsory ideological indoctrination. Children who can hardly utter articulate words are made to sing the praise of Chairman Mao and to chant his quotations. Even science has been completely regimented since the scientists were told in 1952 that "only by joining the masses and cooperating with the Communist Party will scientists be able to find their future."[44]

Because of this gigantic control system the mass line has in practice meant that the masses have always been organized to campaign for the internal and external policies of the party-army complex. In the 'fifties the masses took part in the Three-Anti and Five-Anti campaigns, the Campaign Against Counterrevolutionaries, the Rectification Campaign, the Hu Fang Campaign, the Hundred Flowers Campaign followed by the Anti-Rightist Campaign, the Great Leap Forward, and such other relatively mild campaigns as those to popularize the marriage law, to "increase production and practise economy," and to spread adult literacy. These were followed in the 'sixties by the Socialist Education Movement in the Countryside during which Mao declared that "in the course of the past few months more than a million cadres throughout the country have gone deep down into units at the grass-roots level in the villages, and a new tide has emerged in the movement for socialist revolution,"[45] and the famous Cultural Revolution which convulsed China in the late 'sixties. Even the organization of economic institutions like collective farms and communes was undertaken partly with a view to strengthening and consolidating the political control of the party-army complex over the masses.[46] Finally, culture, the last and generally most inaccessible of the private possessions of the people, has also been fully regimented, any marginal deviations from the "correct line" being "rectified" not only by such phenomena as the Cultural Revolution, but in a less spectacular way by the day-to-day control mechanism of the party-army complex.

It is impossible to explain rationally how, within such a political framework, Mao expects the liberty of the people to be preserved, and such social and economic equality as has been achieved to be meaningful. Nor is it possible to see how he can expect this framework to permit the disappearance of the Communist Party and the state even in the long run. If the masses have any freedom, it is only the freedom to cooperate with the party leadership and to implement the policies and programmes decided by it. Against the background of the history of China in the first half of this century, it is conceivable that the majority of the Chinese people are genuinely loyal to the Communist Party and the government. But this still cannot be called freedom, since the masses who implement the mass line clearly have no other choice. It has sometimes been argued that there was a powerful anarchist element in the Cultural Revolution which was responsible for the virtual transfer of power from the party to the people. Now, although the causes and motivations of the Cultural Revolution were rather complex, involving among other things the personal power of Mao, there can be no doubt that it did in fact seriously undermine the authority of the party. But whether it meant something so revolutionary as the transfer of power to the people is at best extremely doubtful. It was organized not by the people against the party, but by one section of the party headed by Mao, with the help of the army and bands of school students organized as Red Guards, against another. One of its important consequences was the revival and increase of the power and prestige of Mao Tse-tung virtually to the point of deification, and of Lin Piao and the army. It was also an attempt by Mao Tse-tung to rectify rather than abolish the party, which in any case has been largely reorganized, presumably under his guidance, since the end of the Cultural Revolution. In spite of Lin Piao's fall, the party-army complex is still very much the foundation of the Chinese political system, and the apparent shift of power in favour of the army during and after the Cultural Revolution certainly does not indicate an increase in the power of the people.

Gandhi, on the other hand, wanted the constructive programme to function within the framework of a very loose politico-military system. As regards armed forces, it has been already explained that while he seriously believed in the possibility of nonviolent defence against external aggression, he accepted the necessity of maintaining a minimum quantum of armed strength for national defence. The Indian National Congress as an organization did not accept non-violence as a creed even for domestic political purposes, not to speak of external security; and Gandhi did not try to impose his absolute ideals on the organization, as I have stated before. In fact he is said to have supported the dispatch of Indian troops to Kashmir in 1947 to oust the Pakistani raiders. But he was keen that the political system in independent India should not be controlled by the armed forces. He visualized the possibility of a struggle between the civil authorities and the armed forces in independent India, and cautioned against any hegemony or interference on the part of the latter. He also wanted India not to make a drive for military power or to adopt a militaristic stance in her external relations.[47] In other words, the main difference between the Maoist and Gandhian attitudes towards the armed forces is that while the former has accepted and used them on ideological grounds as a major political instrument, operationally indistinguishable from the Communist Party, Gandhi wanted the state to retain a minimum quantum of military power in the background primarily for purposes of external security (in case his prescription for nonviolent defence was not accepted), while the political and social processes went on freely without any operational awareness of the presence of armed forces.

As regards political organization, Gandhi did not regard the Indian National Congress as a political party in the sense in which it is generally understood, namely, an organization primarily if not solely concerned with the seizure and management of political power. In fact, as I have stated before, his conception of politics was highly

idealistic and largely devoid of the idea of power. "Ours is not a
drive for power," he declared categorically, "but merely a nonviolent
fight for India's independence.... A nonviolent soldier of freedom
will covet nothing for himself, he fights only for the freedom of his
country. *The Congress is unconcerned as to who will rule when freedom
is established*."[48] He was distressed by the rapid growth of party
politics in the country shortly before independence and lamented that
the influence of the parties, which was no longer confined to the
cities but had percolated down to the remotest villages, was hindering
the progress of the countryside.[49] When the fight for power started
within the Congress soon after independence, he told his followers in
the organizations of constructive workers: "Today everybody in the
Congress is running after power. That presages grave danger.... It is
my firm view that we should keep altogether aloof from power
politics and its contagion."[50] He also for the first time asked the constructive workers to dissociate themselves in effect, if not formally,
from the political organization of the Indian National Congress.
"Take all the living organizations," he said, "with you. Purify yourselves of all dross. Banish the very idea of capture of power....
Therein lies salvation. There is no other way."[51] So distressed was he
by the political rivalries and the drive for power by individuals and
groups in the Congress, that he exclaimed pathetically: "Thank God,
the Congress is now no longer in sole possession of the field."[52]
Finally, he advised, the day before his assassination, the dissolution
of the Indian National Congress as a political party (which, he
argued, had served its purpose with the attainment of independence)
and its reconstitution as the Lok Sevak Sangh (Servants of People
Society), for which he drafted a constitution under heavy strain
actually on the day of his assassination. The task of this new society,
he said, would be to strive for the attainment of the "social, moral
and economic independence of the seven hundred thousand villages
(this number by implication included the villages in Pakistan). The
following was to be the organizational set-up of the Lok Sevak Sangh
as envisaged by him:

Every panchayat of five adult men or women being villagers,
village-minded, shall form a unit. Two such contiguous panchayats shall form the working party under a leader elected from
among themselves. When there are a hundred such panchayats,

7

the fifty first-grade leaders shall elect from among themselves a second-grade leader and so on, the first-grade leaders meanwhile working under the second-grade leader. Parallel groups of two hundred panchayats shall continue to be formed till they cover the whole of India, each succeeding group of panchayats electing a second-grade leader after the manner of the first. All second-grade leaders shall serve jointly for the whole of India and severally for their respective areas. The second-grade leaders may elect, whenever they deem necessary, from among themselves a chief who will, during pleasure, regulate and command all the groups.[53]

This rather radical prescription was not, however, a sudden inspiration of Gandhi, or caused entirely by the appearance of power politics within the Congress immediately after independence; it flowed more or less logically from his general position that the transformation of civil society was the task of mass action rather than of the state. It was this mass action for which he had organized and led the Congress. He believed strongly in the corrupting influence of power, and argued that "a man who wants to be good and do good in all circumstances must not hold power." He regarded the political education of the masses in the art of nonviolent resistance against the misuse of governmental power as the principal political task, and argued that the good political worker must not go into the legislature himself, but only send his representative. In his own words:

The man of nonviolence can send those to the government who represent his will. If he goes there himself, he exposes himself to the corrupting influence of power. But my representative holds power of attorney only during my pleasure. If he falls a prey to temptation, he can be recalled. I cannot recall myself. All this requires a high degree of intelligence on the part of the electorate. There are about half-a-dozen constructive work organizations. I do not send them to parliament. I want them to keep parliament under check by educating and guiding the voters.[54]

Gandhi himself remained as far away from power as possible for a national leader of his stature. Except once in the early phase, he repeatedly refused to accept the Presidentship of the Congress, and in 1934 resigned even his primary membership of the organization, although continuing to guide the national movement as a whole and the Congress in particular in a purely personal capacity. This is in marked contrast to the record of Mao Tse-tung who took an active part in bitter inner party power struggles for leadership in the early part of his political career and has retained the Chairmanship of the Communist Party all his life. During the crucial years 1946-47, when the struggle for power was going on within the Congress, Gandhi was engaged in a lonesome battle against communal violence throughout the country; and after the independence of India, while all his close followers occupied seats of power, he came nowhere near the corridors of power, although everything would have been his for the mere asking. This attitude was again in sharp contrast to that of Mao who remained President of the People's Republic of China, in addition to being party Chairman, and thus exercised total power personally, until 1959 when he was more or less compelled to give up the Presidentship of the state in favour of Liu Shao Chi mainly on account of the failure of the Great Leap Forward.

Thus it is obvious that the constructive programme is much more consistent with Gandhi's own anarchist utopia with regard to the most fundamental value of an anarchist society, namely, political liberty, than is the mass line with the Marxist-Maoist anarchist utopia, although, as I have pointed out earlier, the low level of technology and material well-being in the Gandhian utopia would make liberty less than perfect. Surely, a process of social transformation which is itself characterized by truly voluntary action on the part of the masses is more creative of liberty than a process which is characterized by a holistic control of the masses by a vast party-army complex which rules in the name of the people. Although the Maoist mass line has probably created greater social equality in China than the Gandhian constructive programme did or could have produced in India, the voluntaristic character of the mass action advocated by Gandhi surely held greater promise of all-round social transformation freely determined by the people than the totalitarian mass control practised in China, which has necessarily prevented the people from deciding anything against the policies and objectives of the Communist Party and from forming any groups or associations not approved by the Communist Party. When the constructive programme is taken together with the other Gandhian instrument of social transformation, namely, satyagraha, whose superiority to people's war as a value-creating means has already been discussed, the Gandhian approach to social transformation as a whole would seem to be more consistent with the ultimate values of liberty, equality and fraternity, subject to the limitations already pointed out. The anarchistic and libertarian content of Gandhism is, therefore, infinitely greater than that of Maoism in which it exists more in name than in reality. It can be broadly stated that both Mao and Gandhi wanted to proceed towards the anarchist utopia by abolishing the distinction between the state and civil society. But while Mao proceeded to do this by absorbing the civil society within the state in a holistic sweep from above, Gandhi's method was that of abolishing the state by the gradual and voluntaristic action of civil society from below. Gandhi's method is definitely more logical than Mao's for moving towards a stateless society.

But it is extremely doubtful whether the element of freedom in the process of social transformation can or should be pushed to the extreme anarchistic limits advocated by Gandhi. In the context of the highly pluralistic and centrifugal pulls characteristic of the Indian socio-political scene, the disbandment of the Indian National Congress, which was the only aggregative political force, would almost certainly have been detrimental to the preservation of that minimum political stability which is a necessary precondition for any kind of ordered national development. In the absence of any organized political force which could perform the task of political aggregation, Indian politics would probably have been highly unstable, almost chaotic, from the beginning of statehood after independence. In terms of strict Gandhian theory, of course, this would not have mattered much, because the Lok Sevak Sangh would have been engaged in transforming the society economically and morally, keeping the politicians under popular control, and maintaining the broader social unity of the country at the non-governmental level. But it seems highly improbable that such an anarchistic attempt would have succeeded in the inherently unstable conditions in partitioned India after independence and in the given international milieu. And this would probably apply to other developing societies as well. Nor should one overemphasize the role of the constructive programme as a determined anarchistic counteroffensive to the power of the state, for the state has an essential role to play in the process of social transformation in a developing society, as I shall explain in the last chapter. The value of the constructive programme lies in its generalized content of social transformation through voluntary and constructive institution-building by the people through corporate self-effort, and as an indicator of the direction in which freedom lies, rather than its specific Gandhian form and Indian context.

CHAPTER FIVE

PROFILES OF PROGRESS

I

THE MAOIST WAY to social transformation has undoubtedly led to major achievements in China. From a historical point of view, the unification of the state under a strong central government has itself been a remarkable achievement and has laid the foundations for China's material progress. The vast apparatus of the Communist Party and its subsidiary organizations, and the periodic mass campaigns led by it, have performed the task of political aggregation and mobilization in a way perhaps never before known in history. The political leadership of Mao and his associates has not only acted as a unifying and stabilizing force, but also created an atmosphere of revolutionary change and a strong desire for forward movement among the masses of the Chinese people. But perhaps the most important achievement from the historico-political point of view has been the spectacular development of the Chinese armed forces which have not only been the basis of the stability and continuity of the new Chinese state, but made her a powerful entity in world affairs. In particular, the systematic development of nuclear weapons including intercontinental ballistic missiles has already made China a potential superpower, at present next only to the USA and the Soviet Union, but capable, in the not too distant future, of posing a serious military challenge even to these two superpowers. What is more important in the Asian context, the growth of military power has enabled China, for the first time in several centuries, to exercise real external sovereignty and to be proudly defiant of the historically imperialist powers and of what the Chinese people as well as millions of other Asians regard as wanton interference by the big powers in the internal affairs of the Afro-Asian states. It was the new-found military strength which enabled Mao to declare with justifiable pride in 1949: "Our nation will never again be an insulted nation. Wę have stood up.... The era in which the Chinese were regarded as uncivilized is now over.... Let the domestic and foreign reactionaries tremble before us."[1] It was a declaration which was, and to this day is, the envy and ambition of many nations of Asia and Africa, and explains largely, in the light of the historical experience of Western imperialism in these countries, the great sympathy and understanding with which millions of people, not only in Asia and Africa but all over the world, view the Maoist model of social transformation in China. The ability of this model to combine the development of a long-term and apparently massive nuclear weapons programme with reasonably rapid economic development has added further to its political attraction in many developing countries.

The economic achievements of the People's Republic of China, though perhaps less breathtaking than its military power, have also been significant. In Marxist theory the unlimited expansion of the forces of production is the primary socio-economic goal, and the revolution is merely a necessary prelude to the release of the forces of production from the shackles imposed on them by the relations of production under capitalism. The institutionalization of the economic system after the revolution is an administrative and relatively unimportant task, and Marx, therefore, left very few details regarding the institutional structure of the Communist economy, except that the entire system of production should be socialized and that the peasants should be given a lot of time to organize agricultural co-operatives on a voluntary basis. But since the Russian Revolution took place in a predominantly agricultural setting and the industrialization of Russia became the main task of the Communist Party, the entire perspective of economic development through Marxism changed radically. It became imperative to raise a large agricultural surplus for investment in industry and to organize agriculture in such a way as would yield the maximum possible agricultural surplus. Moreover, since politics is always in command in Marxism, and the political policy of the Soviet Government was to develop heavy industries (especially armaments industries) at a break-neck pace at the cost of light and consumer goods industries, the generation of the largest possible agricultural surplus and the investment of seventy to seventy-five per cent of the available resources in heavy industry constituted the dominant trend in Soviet economic development. The forced collectivization of agriculture was the principal institutional technique through which the Soviet Government attempted to raise the maximum possible agricultural surplus and which, therefore, constituted the very foundation of Soviet economic development. The rapid economic development of China along Leninist-Stalinist-Maoist lines posed essentially the same kind of problem and required substantially the same type of institutional solution. But in China the problem of rapid industrialization was much more difficult, since the country was industrially much less developed and much more populous than Russia at the time of the Revolution. The institutional and organizational effort required for the economic development of China, therefore, had to be much greater than in Russia; and this is the fundamental problem which Mao has solved to a considerable extent by applying the mass line for the institutional reorganization and decentralized development of the Chinese economy. The successful implementation of land reforms and the rehabilitation of the war-torn economy within three years after the revolution were significant achievements. The collectivization and attempted communization of agriculture, whatever their actual effects on agricultural production may have been, have helped the state to establish full control over the hitherto unorganized peasant population, and probably also (if the Soviet example is any guide) to extract a larger surplus from agriculture for the purpose of industrialization than would otherwise have been possible. The industrial sector has been characterized not only by the establishment of complete state hegemony, but also by rapid growth of production, especially in the armaments and other related heavy industries like steel, as in the Soviet Union. Through periodic mass campaigns and the inculcation of the new values of discipline, frugality and sacrifice, an unprecedented economic mobilization and a forward momentum have been achieved. But perhaps most important of all, science and technology have received a tremendous impetus under the Communist regime, and the scientific spirit has been deliberately inculcated among the masses, with consequences which are destined to be far-reaching.

The traditional class structure of Chinese society has been seriously undermined, and although according to Mao the class struggle in China will continue for several centuries, there can be little doubt about the validity of his claim that the old exploiting classes have by and large been eliminated. The traditional Chinese family has undergone considerable change, there has been a drastic alteration and widening of its functions, and a serious assault has been made on its inner structure. Through regular mass campaigns and propagation of new social values a massive social mobilization has been achieved, which, both in intensity and extent, is probably unparalleled in the history of the world, with the only exception of a comparable achievement by Gandhi in pre-independence India. But perhaps most important of all, mass education and literacy have undergone a phenomenal expansion under the Communist regime, which is bound to have a revolutionary impact on the organization and outlook of the Chinese society in the long run.

Thus Mao's China has definitely made rapid progress towards the building of a powerful state system. But we must ask ourselves the fundamental question, to what extent have the achievements of China under the leadership of Mao Tse-tung led to, or can be logically expected to lead to, an approximation to the value-goal of Marxism characterized by liberty, equality and fraternity for society as a whole, which in fact constitutes the internal theoretical justification for the entire Marxist-Maoist scheme of social engineering?

In discussing the problem of values in connection with a political system it must be remembered, first of all, that values relate to human lives and that, therefore, the loss of life, if any, involved in the process by which a system comes into existence and then sustains itself is a matter of fundamental importance. From this point of view, the Communist political model is undoubtedly the costliest model of the twentieth century. Even in the Soviet Union where the loss of life in the Revolution of 1917 was negligible, the loss of life in the subsequent period has been placed at several million by the most conservative estimates. In China Mao declared as early as 1927 that "it was necessary to bring about a brief reign of terror in every rural area, else one could never suppress the activities of the counterrevolutionaries in the countryside or overthrow the authority of the gentry."[2] Apart from this terror, the prolonged civil war which brought the Communist Party to power itself took a very heavy toll in human lives. It is also a well-known fact that the first decade of Communist rule in China witnessed large-scale liquidations resulting from opposition to the political and economic policies of the government. In 1957 Mao declared that "our success in suppressing counterrevolu-

tionaries is undoubtedly an important reason for the consolidation
of the state," and explained one of the methods by which this was
done. "After liberation," he said, "we rooted out a number of
counterrevolutionaries. Some were sentenced to death for major
crimes. This was absolutely necessary, it was the demand of the
broad masses of the people, it was done to free the masses from long
years of oppression by the counterrevolutionaries and all kinds of
local tyrants; in other words, it was done to liberate the productive
forces."[3] There is a good deal of evidence to indicate that not only
during the first decade, but also in the periodic mass campaigns which
took place subsequently, a huge loss of life resulted directly from the
policy of suppression followed by the Communist Party and its
government. According to official Soviet estimates, 26.4 million
people were "exterminated" in China between 1949 and 1965,
2.8 million during 1949-52 (i.e. during the period of land reform
and political "rectification"), 3.6 million during 1953-57 (i.e. during
the period of collectivization), 6.7 million during 1958-60 (i.e. during
the period of communization), and 13.3 million during 1961-65.[4]
According to the estimate of *New York Times*, 30 million people were
exterminated in the first decade of Communist rule in China.[5] There
are various other similar estimates, but the latest and most com-
prehensive estimate is that of Professor Richard Walker, Director,
Institute of International Studies, University of South Carolina, who
has prepared a minimum and a maximum estimate of loss of life in
China from 1927 to 1970 which, in his opinion, can be directly attributed to the Communist Party's drive for power from 1927 to 1949
and Communist rule since 1949, on the basis of all available primary
and secondary sources, including official Chinese sources. According
to the minimum estimate, the total number of killings during the
entire period was 34.3 million, and according to the maximum estimate 63.78 million. But Walker has unreasonably included the
Chinese casualties in the Sino-Japanese War and the Korean War in
these estimates. If the relevant figures pertaining to these wars are
omitted, the minimum and maximum estimates come to 33.75 million
and 62.5 million respectively.[6] The minimum figure is consistent with
the Soviet estimate of 26.4 million exterminations up to 1965. Even
if these figures are assumed to be grossly exaggerated, the number of
exterminations carried out by the Communist Party and government
in China must be a staggering figure of many millions.

The other major method of suppressing "counterrevolutionaries" which has always been openly admitted and even proudly declared by the People's Government is "reform through labour." One Western scholar estimated the number of political prisoners in labour camps at about 14 million in 1954.[7] A UNESCO report of 1955 estimated that 20 to 25 million people were in regular camps and another 12.5 million in corrective labour camps.[8] According to official Soviet estimates, in 1967 there were over 18 million political prisoners in 10,000 labour camps in China.[9]

As regards the political system itself, the Marxian argument in support of the dictatorship of the proletariat is mainly two-fold, namely, that it is a dictatorship of a vast majority over a small minority of the people; and that it is merely transitional in character. The second part of the argument has been largely refuted by Mao himself, as noted earlier. In his view, the socialization of production is only one of the conditions necessary for the abolition of class distinctions and hence of the proletarian dictatorship; and class struggle at the political, ideological and cultural levels must go on indefinitely, at least for several centuries. To him, therefore, the abolition of the classes, the withering away of the state, and the approximate realization of the ultimate values represent a very distant goal, not only because of the existence of "international imperialism," but more importantly, of fundamental inner contradictions within the socialist society. The two factors, external and internal, combine to make the social goal so very remote in Mao's thought as to deprive it of any practical significance for the generations of the present and the immediate future. Besides, by admitting the process to be reversible, Mao has in fact seriously undermined the historical inevitability of the Marxian social goal and virtually abandoned the teleological justification for the dictatorship of the proletariat.

The only practical Maoist justification for the form of government established in China under his leadership is that it is a dictatorship of the vast majority of the people, for their own good, over a small minority, and is an end in itself for that reason, irrespective of what happens in the distant future. Apart from the question whether values can be measured quantitatively, this argument is vitiated by the simple fact that the Communist form of government which has developed since the Russian Revolution, whether it is called a People's Democratic Dictatorship or a "state of the whole people" (as

Khrushchev tried to characterize the Soviet Union at the 22nd Congress of the CPSU), is run by a totalitarian party, the Communist Party, which is merely a self-appointed trustee rather than a freely chosen representative of the people and which comes to power and remains there primarily through the force of arms. Undoubtedly, no Communist Party in power relies on force alone; the vast party machine is geared to a massive propaganda effort and indoctrination campaign in order to persuade the people in favour of the government and its policies. This has been particularly true in the case of the Chinese government, mainly on account of the great emphasis laid by Mao on the mass line in party-work, and especially on regular mass campaigns. Yet when all is said, the vast party-army complex in China exercises a holistic control over the political, economic, social and cultural life of the people which it is beyond their power to reject or even to modify. The party organization itself is theoretically characterized by "democratic centralism," but Mao has tried (like Lenin, Stalin and other Communist leaders) to resolve the contradiction between democracy and centralism by decreeing that the latter prevails over the former, thus making it possible for an unprecedented and hitherto inconceivable personality cult to manifest itself in China, as it did earlier in the Soviet Union. The result is that what appears as a tremendous mass mobilization from one point of view seems from another to be the establishment of total political control by the Communist Party over the entire population, since every school, every factory, every institution and every mass organization is in fact controlled by party activists according to Mao's "three-in-one" principle of organization. What from one point of view appears to be the mobilization of the peasants into new types of agricultural organization, may be regarded from another point of view as the imposition on the peasants, against their will, of a system which is totally opposed to the promises on the basis of which the party had earlier secured their cooperation for capturing power. What is scientific, industrial and technological progress from one point of view is the strengthening of the regime through the achievement of its political goals from another. What is mass education in one sense is mass indoctrination in another. Finally, what is a vast social mobilization from one point of view is, from another, the attempt of the party to reach the last and most inaccessible region of its holistic control, namely, the social and cultural life of the people.

But if the argument is vitiated by the nature of the political system, it is nevertheless not altogether lost. The Chinese people have undoubtedly lost their liberty in the sense that they cannot freely decide the nature of their political, economic and social systems, the direction, priorities and patterns of change, or even the contours of their personal social and cultural lives. According to many defenders of liberty, this loss is so fundamental that it cannot be compensated by any other gains in human life, material or otherwise. But revolutions and their consequences have to be studied and assessed in a historical perspective, and, in the context of Chinese history, the gains accompanying the loss of liberty on the part of the masses of Chinese people have been far from insignificant, even in terms of values. When one looks at the history of imperialism in Asia and Africa, the pathetic and very terrible degradation and suffering of untold millions under the weight of superior Western military force, the external security and respectability gained by China by virtue of her sheer military power and political stability can be seen as the winning of a collective external liberty on the part of the Chinese people which is a necessary precondition to their internal liberty. As regards equality, the virtual destruction of the traditional class structure of Chinese society, the inculcation of the spirit of frugality, diligence and sacrifice among all sections of people including the political leadership, the glorification of labour, the spread of mass education and culture, price control, rationing, forms of social security including a national health programme—have all been part of a social levelling which does represent a certain real form of equality. If it is true that equality is seriously incomplete without liberty, which is a political and, therefore, inclusive form of equality, it is equally true that liberty in the absence of socio-economic equality is grossly inadequate. So far as fraternity is concerned, it would be correct to say that the process of socio-economic levelling, combined with mass mobilization and the inculcation of revolutionary consciousness, does represent an attempt on the part of the party and the government to induce fraternal feelings among the majority of the people. But at the same time the fundamentally compulsive and violent methods adopted for the resolution of social contradictions, especially in the light of the more or less arbitrary distinction between the "people" and their "enemies" according to time and circumstances, makes it extremely doubtful whether real fraternity can ever be established in the Maoist state where, according to Mao himself, social contradictions would be permanent. All that can be definitely said with regard to the Marxist-Maoist approach to fraternity is that its main if not only contribution lies in pointing attention to the socio-economic basis of this ultimate value.

Besides, if material progress is a necessary precondition for the realization of the ultimate values, the merits of the Maoist model of social transformation must be judged also in the light of its relative efficiency in achieving the rapid industrialization of a predominantly agricultural and populous country with relatively rigid social traditions. Indeed, the appeal of Marxism in Asia rests today not so much on the Marxian philosophy of history and prognosis of capitalism as on its supposed efficacy as an ideology of industrialization. Since the success of the Soviet Union in transforming itself from a backward agricultural country into a modern industrial one under the impact of Marxism as interpreted by Lenin and Stalin, Asian Marxist intellectuals have tended to regard Marxism mainly as a short-cut to economic development and national power. The relative success of China with regard to industrialization within a short period of time under the leadership of Mao Tse-tung has strengthened the belief of many intellectuals in Asia and elsewhere that the Soviet and Chinese type of forced industrialization (and hence the Marxist ideology which inspired it) is the most "scientific" path open before the economically underdeveloped countries of the world. The first requirement of such countries, before one can meaningfully talk about the liberty, equality and fraternity of the masses, so runs the argument, is material betterment which can come only through rapid industrialization. The Soviet and Chinese method of industrialization, it is argued, has been demonstrated to be the quickest one, and hence it is rational for the underdeveloped countries to accept this method. It is admitted that this method is compulsive in nature; but it is argued that every method of industrialization has its own costs. The industrialization of the Western countries involved, among other things, the exploitation and pauperization of the working class which was sharply emphasized by Marx. Liberal democratic methods of development in populous agricultural societies steeped in traditional mores would cause inordinate delay, and the human cost of development under this system in the form of the prolonged poverty of the masses would be more than that of the Soviet-Chinese method. The validity of the argument that the Communist method of forced industrialization is the most efficient one for the economically under-developed countries is not accepted by all (it is in fact disproved by the Japanese and the East European examples) and I shall discuss it subsequently. But it is necessary to note here that in so far as it is one of the most important models of rapid industrialization, the argu-ments of those who are attracted by it cannot be lightly brushed aside.

At this stage, however, it is necessary to realize that although the Maoist approach to social transformation has not been entirely counterproductive of the ultimate values in China, neither can its contributions to these values be regarded as Marxian. Marx had visualized the liberty of each individual resulting from the withering away of the apparatus of the state, which was to him by definition an instrument of terror, and not the virtual elimination of individual liberty by a compulsive, growing, and self-perpetuating party-state even for the sake of external security. The equality envisioned by him was not the arbitrary equality imposed from above by a powerful and self-perpetuating party-state, but the spontaneous equality following from the socialization of production and the disappearance of the state. The fraternity he believed in was also to follow from the dis-appearance of classes, and not the dubious fraternity of the masses of people mobilized by the party-state, on pain of extermination or "reform through labour," for dealing with class contradictions over several centuries.

Moreover, it is easy to see that the Maoist transformation of China, like the Leninist-Stalinist transformation of Russia, has not led to the emergence of a society which is wholly different from *the civilization* of the Western world which Marx wanted to replace completely with the exception of its technological base. The nuclear-armed Soviet state with virtually unlimited power within and an attitude of dominance and challenge towards the rest of the world is, in terms of power, only a superior version of the Prussian state and its contemporary equivalents which Marx was out to destroy, and in no way different from the hated Western powers. The drive for in-dustrialization has led to the growth of an industrial bureaucracy and of the acquisitive ethos of a consumer economy which are different from their Western counterparts, if at all, only in degree. Even the industrial management and pricing system of the Soviet Union, along

with other economic aspects of the great convergence, has started resembling the Western pattern in several important respects. In China,
while these tendencies have not developed to the same proportions
as in the Soviet Union, due to the tremendous head start of the latter,
there can be no doubt that they have been growing rapidly. Mao is
obviously aware of the strength of these tendencies, as is evident from
the fact that one of the major aspects of the Cultural Revolution was
a determined assault on bureaucratization and "economism," but
whether the mass line can radically alter the consequences of the
industrialization and power drive seems at best doubtful. Even with
regard to the all-important question of the resolution of contradictions, the difference between the Maoist state and the Western states
is one of degree rather than of kind. So far as internal contradictions
are concerned, while the Western states seek to resolve them through
the legal and administrative apparatus of the state, in China the
party-state tries to resolve contradictions by going one step further
and mobilizing the masses in support of its policies through a combination of compulsion, persuasion and indoctrination. The difference is even less with regard to external contradictions, for while
Mao lays such great ideological stress on people's war, Maoist China,
like the Soviet Union, has in practice been increasingly dependent on
a massive nuclear weapons programme in no way different from that
of the USA.

Neither the nonfulfilment of the Marxian value-goals nor the increasing approximation of the Soviet and Chinese models to their
Western counterparts can, however, be regarded as mere accidents of
history; they are in fact in some vital ways the logical outcome of
the inner contradictions of the Marxist approach to social transformation. For social contradictions cannot be resolved and liberty,
equality and fraternity truly established through the violent suppression of one of the elements in the contradiction by another. This
process merely perpetuates and escalates the contradiction, as Gandhi
and many others have rightly argued. When a class or any other
group seizes the state through violence, it inevitably sets up a violent
regime, in the first place because of the simple socio-psychological fact
that the violence perpetrated by its members conditions their subsequent behaviour; and secondly because they prepare themselves for
violent defence against actual and potential reprisals from those
whom they have suppressed, since that is the only form of defence

they know and are used to. A successful class struggle, whose immediate objective is the seizure of the state, would lead inevitably, therefore, to a dictatorship of the victorious class, as Marx had correctly concluded. Moreover, this dictatorship was bound to be "unrestrained by law and based on force," as Stalin rightly argued. But Marx was wrong in assuming that the dictatorship and the state under its control would rapidly wither away once the relations of production were transformed through the socialization of production. Contrary to what Marx thought, social contradictions are not caused by exploitative relations of production alone, but also by a variety of other factors including the desire for power and other "basic urges," race, language, religion, culture, nationality and the colour of the skin. Hence, even in an international system in which production has been socialized, neither the internal nor the external contradictions of a state are likely to disappear. New forms of contradiction would inevitably develop and perpetuate the dictatorship, the state and the violence it represents. That is why the dictatorship of the proletariat in the Soviet Union, even fifty-five years after the Revolution, still finds itself unable to permit such minimum liberties as the writing of pacifist poetry and historical novels on the pre-revolutionary period, not to speak of free political organization and expression of opinion. That is why new privileged classes have appeared in the Soviet Union, as pointed out by the Yugoslav Communist leader, Milovan Djilas, and more importantly by Mao himself. According to Mao: "The members of this privileged stratum have converted the function of serving the masses into the privilege of dominating them. They... appropriate the fruits of the Soviet people's labour and pocket incomes that are dozens or even a hundred times those of the average Soviet worker and peasant.... Completely divorced from the working people of the Soviet Union, they live the parasitical and decadent life of the bourgeoisie.... Their sole concern is to consolidate their economic position and political rule."[10] "International imperialism" may to some extent explain the external posture of the Soviet Union, but it certainly cannot explain the internal political system it seems determined to perpetuate. That is also why major contradictions have developed among the Communist states themselves, although all of them have established the dictatorship of the proletariat and socialized production. Considering the military birth of the People's Republic of China and the

8

essentially compulsive character of its political system, it is unlikely to develop differently from the Soviet model, in spite of the Cultural Revolution and other similar future revolutions promised by Mao.

Nor is it surprising that the violent method of social transformation has resulted in the approximation of the actual Communist models to their Western counterparts, for the idea that violence can be cured by violence is a misconception that Marx derived from the actual practice of the Western states and societies. He was shocked by the reactionary, oppressive and violent character of the European states in the eighteenth and nineteenth centuries and saw the way out in a modified version of the French Revolution, the peasant uprisings in France and Germany, the European revolution of 1848, and the Paris Commune. He saw that none of these uprisings led to the establishment of liberty, equality and fraternity, although they were otherwise of major historical significance, but mistakenly believed that this was because state power had not been effectively captured and production socialized. Mao learnt his famous thesis that political power grows out of the barrel of the gun not only from his Marxist inheritance, but also from the fact that Western political power appeared on the Chinese shores in the 19th century in the form of gunboats rather than enlightenment and humanism. The imitation of this essentially Western method for resolving internal and external contradictions, be it in Russia, China or elsewhere, logically involves also the need for imitating the industrial and military power of the West.

But the totalitarian and self-perpetuating character of the Communist regimes, including the Chinese, is ultimately traceable to the Hegelian ancestry of Marxism with regard to the belief in historical inevitability. To Hegel's metaphysical notion of the inevitable teleological movement of history Marx added a social content and an element of conscious human cooperation. Man's task lies in recognizing the necessity and inevitability of the historical process, characterized by the class struggle, the revolution (at the end of capitalist development), the dictatorship of the proletariat and the disappearance of classes and the state; and in consciously accelerating this inevitable movement and consummation of history. It is the determination of some men to keep history on this preconceived and unchangeable course which impels them to control other human beings through violence and tyranny, whose free actions might otherwise deflect history from its preordained course.

The importance of Marxism for the transformation of economically backward societies lies not in its philosophy of history, nor in its theory of armed revolution and dictatorship of the proletariat. It lies rather in the ideology's emphasis on science, technology and the unlimited productive possibilities (largely borrowed by Marx from Saint-Simon); its opposition to religious and other superstitions; its insistence on the ability of the deprived masses to split their rails and make their own history; and finally, its epoch-making and palpably valid assertion that the achievement of liberty, equality and fraternity requires a fundamental reconstruction of socio-economic relations rather than a mere change of government or a modification of the legal and constitutional apparatus of the state. Mao Tse-tung has applied his Marxian inheritance in these respects to the transformation of China. His additional personal contribution lies in that he has pragmatically related his political, economic and social ideas to the requirements of a traditional peasant society and galvanized the peasantry into a great instrument of change; shown a way to mass mobilization without which it would be impossible to bring about rapid socio-economic change in the populous agricultural countries; demonstrated the pragmatic necessity in such countries of economic decentralization, for the effective utilization of the vast manpower potential, for economic development and for removing the contradiction between the city and the village; emphasized the need for direct and organized action on the part of the masses in order not only to alter socio-economic relations, but also to purify the state system continuously; recognized and openly admitted the inevitability of the indefinite continuance of the state and the party-dictatorship under Marxism-Leninism; seen the possibility of new classes, bureaucratic tendencies and the acquisitive spirit developing in the course of industrialization even after the socialization of production; and insisted on the need for a conscious, deliberate and subjective effort on the part of the individual to transform his social consciousness perpetually, even after the establishment of socialism. The question is whether these positive aspects of the Maoist model can be separated from its politico-military aspects and combined with an essentially libertarian political system for the rapid transformation of a populous agricultural society.

II

Compared with the Maoist model of social transformation, the Gandhian model is weak with respect to the building of state power. In the political sphere, although Gandhi built up a mass political party mainly based on the peasantry which aggregated and articulated the multiplicity of interests involved in the Indian freedom movement, acted as the principal organizational instrument of the struggle against British imperialism, functioned as a vehicle of social transformation, and has given a high degree of stability and continuity to the Indian state system since independence, it was and still is a much weaker party than the Chinese Communist Party in terms of political power. Before India's independence, although this party succeeded in achieving a spectacular political mobilization, especially through the mass movements, its utterly nonviolent character, lack of any rigid ideology and organized indoctrination, basis in consensus and loose organization made it a kind of political platform which was much weaker in terms of political power than the Communist Party built by Mao. Gandhi's anarchistic determination to keep the Congress out of power politics in independent India did not succeed, but the legacy he left behind has made the Congress after independence infinitely weaker as a political force than the Communist Party of China. The absence of any direct link between it and the armed forces, the broad nature of its ideology, its relatively loose organizational character and lack of any machinery for organized indoctrination, the freedom of other parties and organizations to agitate against it and to challenge it freely in elections, and the general constitutional framework within which it functions, all go to make it an incomparably weaker instrument of political control than Mao's party.

The legacy of Gandhi has also been partly responsible for making independent India a militarily weaker state than China. India constitutes practically a solitary exception to the general pattern of the armed forces exercising governmental power, periodically if not constantly, in the newly independent states of Asia and Africa. It is also one of the few countries in the modern world which does not have a system of compulsory military service. Although various other factors have probably contributed to this political development in India, there can be very little doubt that the nonviolent character of the national movement led by Gandhi and the general renunciation of military methods by the Indian national movement for both internal and external purposes contributed greatly to the relegation of the armed forces to a secondary position after independence. Moreover, if independent India has not made a drive for becoming a major military power, through universal military training and a lopsided investment in armaments; if it has refused to manufacture nuclear weapons for many years in spite of possessing the necessary technical know-how and material resources, this must be traced at least partly to the influence of Gandhi, as the official statements of Prime Minister Nehru and his successors as well as the nuclear weapons debate in India in general would indicate. Similarly, there can be little doubt that India's policy of nonalignment and her opposition to military alliances have been considerably influenced by the Gandhian way of thinking on defence and international relations.[11]

In the economic sphere, while the government leaders in independent India did not share the broad Gandhian bias against "industrialism" and rapid technological advance, the programme of economic development adopted by them has been basically tempered by the Gandhian view of industrialization as a means to the construction of a society representing certain ultimate values rather than an end in itself, even in the short run. Thus agriculture has been treated, not as a kind of colony to be squeezed to the uttermost limit for the sake of the maximum possible rate of industrialization, but as a relatively independent sector of the economy which, though vital to industrialization, must be treated tenderly for the sake of the overwhelming majority of people as well as for preserving the value-structure aimed at. Instead of the collective farms and communes of China, which have been used primarily for establishing the total control of the party on the millions of small farmers, restricting agricultural consumption to the barest minimum, and thus extracting the maximum possible agricultural surplus, in India an attempt has been made to improve agriculture through such Gandhian and quasi-Gandhian institutions as *panchayeti raj*, Community Development and agricultural co-operation, in addition to land reforms through legislative and administrative means. In the industrial sector, the same value-oriented approach has led to the adoption of a pattern of democratic planning, broadly supported by Gandhi, in which an attempt has been made to secure a relatively balanced development of light and consumer goods industries on the one hand and heavy industries on the other, rather than to secure the maximum possible development of the latter at the cost of the former, as in the Soviet Union and China. Hence although the rate of economic development in India has been on the whole comparable to that of China,[12] the latter has probably developed a stronger infrastructure of heavy industries and consequently a stronger power base for the state than India.

As regards socio-cultural change, education has undergone rapid expansion at all levels. Primary education has been made free and universal, as was desired by Gandhi, although the Gandhian scheme of basic education has not been accepted. Higher education has expanded rapidly, and in particular, there has been a phenomenal expansion of higher education in science, technology, medicine and engineering. The financial and human resources invested in scientific research and development, including the peaceful uses of atomic energy, have increased many times since independence.[13] Although this has meant a certain departure from the basic Gandhian approach to science and technology, it is consistent with the value-oriented transformation of a developing society, as I have argued before. So far as social stratification is concerned, the Indian constitution, which was drafted by Dr B. R. Ambedkar, the leader of the untouchables, has abolished untouchability and made it a punishable offence, established equality before law for all citizens regardless of caste, race, religion or sex, and reserved seats in the parliament and state assemblies as well as in government service for the formerly depressed castes. But here again, the essentially libertarian character of the state has made it a relatively weak instrument of social control and prevented it from implementing its policies in practice as effectively as in China. And finally, the state has displayed neither the desire nor the power to control the cultural life of the people.

The relatively weak power base of India as compared to that of the People's Republic of China is of course a merit rather than a defect from the point of view of the ultimate values, in so far as this is an inevitable corollary of the fundamental freedoms which circumscribe the power of the state in India in theory as well as in practice, and can be directly traced to the ideological character of the national movement led by Gandhi. While it is true that the state can and often does play a creative role with regard to the realization of liberty, equality and fraternity in the process of social transformation, for example, by regulating economic activity, freeing the individual from the communal tyranny of a traditional society, and in general by trying to conciliate these values into a dynamic equilibrium, it is equally true that an unrestricted growth of state power has almost always led to tyranny within and war without. The viability and external security of a state in the modern world also demand that it must have a minimum quantum of political, military and economic power, but there is a distinction of kind rather than of degree between regarding this minimum power as unavoidable for practical purposes, as Gandhi did, and treating it as more or less an end in itself. There can be very little doubt that a process of development which is marked by definite safeguards against an unlimited expansion of state power is more consistent with the ultimate values than one in which the distinction between the state and civil society is obliterated in a holistic sweep and the internal as well as external power of the state continues to grow indefinitely. It is for this reason that Bertrand Russell preferred the Indian model of value-oriented politico-economic development to the Marxist-Maoist totalitarian model. Said Russell:

India has been launched upon a regime of parliamentary democracy—a difficult feat, as may be seen in many different parts of the world where attempts have been made to substitute New Democracy for old imperialism. The second great task in which the Nehru Government has been engaged is that of introducing industrialism without the harsh features that have usually been associated with its early stages. The cruelties of industrialism in Britain in the early nineteenth century are a familiar theme, and everyone knows that Marx's doctrines were inspired by horror of what was occurring in British factories when Marx was young. It is one of the remarkable ironies of history that, as soon as Marxists acquired power in Russia, they proceeded to inflict, on a much larger scale, evils very similar to those which shocked their prophet. Early industrialism has been associated with hardship everywhere except in the northern States of America which could draw upon a destitute immigrant population for whose poverty America was not responsible. In India, Nehru's Government is content to let the process of industrializing be somewhat slower than in contemporary China in order that the process may be less painful and less harsh. Every humane person should sympathize with this endeavour and should realize that the outcome, even if it takes longer, is likely to be better in terms of human happiness than the outcome of a less humane process.[14]

But free India has largely failed to achieve the mass mobilization for political, economic and socio-cultural change which both Mao and Gandhi have rightly regarded as an imperative necessity for a populous agricultural society in the process of development, and which Gandhi tried to synthesize with a nonviolent and libertarian political system. In the political sphere, although the five general elections and numerous local and state elections as well as the general process of democratic political development have necessarily involved extensive mass participation in politics, the foundations of political self-government in the villages, which Gandhi rightly considered to be the first prerequisite to the free political mobilization of the masses within the framework of democracy, are yet to be properly laid. Gandhi advocated the revival of the traditional institution of village *panchayet* (government by five elected persons) for imparting a widely participatory character to democracy in free India. Village *swaraj* (self-government) was to be the political framework within which the constructive work for rural development was to take place. He wanted Indian independence to "begin at the bottom," and each village *panchayet* to have full administrative, financial and judicial powers. Since the constructive programme would involve the attempt on the part of the villagers to eradicate untouchability, casteism, communalism, illiteracy, and economic and social inequality, the village *panchayet* in free India would obviously be radically different from its traditional form.[15] The government of free India did not try to implement this programme until the inadequacy of popular participation in the Community Development Programme became glaring. Thereafter it introduced a broad programme of *panchayeti raj* at the village, development bloc and district levels. Although this institutional change has achieved a measure of success from the point of view of popular participation in rural development,[16] it has not gone nearly as far as Gandhi had envisaged, due to two main reasons. First, in the absence of the mass movements visualized by Gandhi, rural self-government has been vitiated by casteism, communalism, untouchability and other social contradictions. Secondly, in many states the institutions of self-government at various levels have been given merely nominal financial and administrative powers; and even in those states where relatively extensive powers have been given under the law, the divisions among the villagers have in practice resulted in concentration of most of the powers in the hands of the bureaucracy.

The net result of the failure to maintain the momentum of mass participation in politics initiated by Gandhi has been that democracy in India is largely characterized by the rule of the bureaucracy. This bureaucracy, moreover, has inherited practically all the characteristics and administrative procedures of the British Indian bureaucracy, and no visible attempt has been made to change its character in the new situation. Although some bureaucracies of Asia and Africa are probably less competent and more corrupt than their Indian counterpart, it is doubtful whether any other bureaucracy in the world enjoys the prestige and power of the Indian bureaucracy. While this development would not probably have been harmful beyond a certain limit in a politically and economically developed and stable country, for a populous new democracy in the process of economic development, which requires mass mobilization on an extensive scale, it is far from satisfactory. It is precisely for this reason that the anti-bureaucratic character of the mass movements launched by Mao in China, of which the Cultural Revolution was only a major example, has a great and understandable appeal to a certain section of the Indian youth and intelligentsia.

In the economic sphere, Mao has been more successful in continuing the application of the "guerilla methods" of production, characteristic of the Yenan days, to the economic development of the People's Republic of China, than the followers of Gandhi have been in India in continuing to apply the "satyagrahi methods" of the constructive workers to the economic development of independent India. The Community Development Programme, which was started in 1952 and now covers the entire country, was at least partly Gandhian in inspiration, in so far as it was based on the principle of 50 per cent contribution by the government and 50 per cent by the people— 25 per cent in money and 25 per cent in labour. Originally its aim was also to bring about a radical transformation in the whole structure of the rural society along Gandhian lines, rather than the mere improvement of agricultural production. But because the Indian National Congress did not take up the challenge of mass mobilization after independence, which alone could have ensured the desired mass participation in the Community Development Programme, and no other mass organization came forward to perform this task, very soon the programme drifted almost entirely into the hands of the bureaucracy and remained a programme of the masses only in name. For all practical purposes it became a programme for the masses organized and operated by the bureaucracy.[17] The attempt to link the Community Development Programme to the institution of *panchayeti raj* or local self-government in the villages has also not been particularly successful, because in the absence of effective mass mobilization, *panchayeti raj* itself has proved to be largely a bureaucratic endeavour, at least in the majority of the Indian states. There are obvious difficulties in mass mobilization with a common focus in a multi-party democracy; but the important point is that the attempt at mass mobilization for economic development has not at all been made either by the ruling party or by any other party or mass organization. Gandhi alone had visualized the need for an organization for such mass mobilization in free India and, therefore, suggested the organization of a Lok Sevak Sangh in place of the Indian National Congress. And if it is true, as the Planning Commission says in India's *Fourth Five-Year Plan*, that in spite of all these limitations the Community Development Programme has substantially changed the face of the Indian villages,[18] this success must at least partly be attributed to the Gandhian accent on the development of the Indian villages.

The only unofficial organization which has made some attempt at constructive work under Gandhian inspiration is the Akhil Bharat Sarva Seva Sangh (which is responsible for the Sarvodaya Movement, including the Bhoodan and Gramdan movements) led by Acharya Vinoba Bhave and Jayaprakash Narayan. But the Sarvodaya leaders have not been particularly successful in mobilizing the masses for economic development and social transformation for various important reasons. In the first place, they have not been able to adapt their detailed programmes to contemporary economic conditions. A quarter century after the independence of India they are still insisting on retaining the spinning wheel as the principal instrument of economic development, instead of developing more modern and productive handicrafts and small-scale industries; there is a debate among the leaders even now as to whether electricity should be introduced in the villages. Secondly, their activities depend on heavy governmental subsidy (contrary to Gandhi's thinking on the subject) rather than the self-help of the masses. Thirdly, so far as the Bhoodan movement is concerned, they have merely been requesting the landowners to surrender a very small part of their land, and not launched any satyagraha anywhere in India against big landowners or other vested interests. Finally, no attempt has been made to attack the stratified social structure of the village as a whole. It must be realized, however, that the work of the Sarvodaya Movement and its leaders has not been entirely in vain. Away from the struggles of party politics, they have at least succeeded in keeping alive the psychology of constructive work and an equalitarian moral atmosphere in the Indian villages.

One major consequence of the inability of the government, political parties and voluntary organizations to mobilize the masses for decentralized economic development has been the partial failure of such vital institutional changes in agriculture as land reforms and cooperation. The adoption of correct policies and the establishment of legal and bureaucratic procedures are by themselves grossly inadequate for the institutional reorganization of a populous peasant society which inevitably requires a mass movement at the grassroot level. In the absence of such a mass movement the land reforms and the cooperative movement, though correct in their libertarian and egalitarian perspectives, have in practice been only partially successful. Moreover, such vital constructive endeavour as the construction of medium and small irrigation projects, cottage and small-scale industries, etc. has lacked the pace and momentum that only mass participation can impart to it, and the bureaucratic effort to implement rationally conceived measures in this sphere has met with very limited success.

Another vital economic consequence of the absence of mass mobilization has been the failure to reduce economic inequality. From all accounts, the gap between the rich and the poor has continued to increase in independent India, and new privileged classes, including a rapidly growing bureaucracy, have appeared in the midst of acute poverty. Even the new political elite in independent India has assumed the character of a highly privileged class. In this vital sphere the "followers" of Gandhi who came to power in 1947 failed signally to follow their austere leader. While the palaces of the former Chinese emperors were converted into museums by the Communist leaders of China, the first Indian Governor-General and then the first President of the Republic of India moved promptly into the palace of the

British Viceroy; the first Prime Minister of India moved into the palace formerly used by the British Commander-in-Chief of the Indian armed forces; the other Ministers occupied the best available houses in the capital; and a period of ostentatious living and great pomp and show all round began immediately at the higher political levels. This process was naturally repeated in the provinces; and the bureaucracy throughout the country understandably emulated the example of their political masters. All this time the hovels of the poor, which Gandhi had declared would not exist in independent India for a single day, not only continued to exist but also to multiply in the vast slums of Delhi, Calcutta, Bombay, Madras, Lucknow, and in the hundreds of thousands of Indian villages. A vast socio-economic gap between the masses on the one hand and the political elite and bureaucrats on the other has thus continued to develop in independent India, which constitutes, along with the growing inequality between the more traditional economic classes, a standing negation of the ethos of an egalitarian society.

The effects in the socio-cultural sphere have been equally grave. Adult education, which is vital for mass participation in the process of development in a predominantly illiterate society, and to which Gandhi attached such great importance, has received a relatively low priority in the educational policy of the government, and the attempt to implement this policy through bureaucratic methods rather than through mass mobilization has prevented it from making any visible impact on the illiterate masses of India. Even primary education which is free and universal in theory is in fact far from universal, for although it has been declared to be compulsory, the state neither can nor should penalize defaulting parents; and the solution lies again in mass mobilization which has been missing from the Indian political scene in the post-Gandhian period. The net result is that approximately 70 per cent of India's population still remains illiterate a quarter century after independence. Nor has the spirit of science, in this situation, made any dent on the age-old religious superstitions and social prejudices of the people. As regards higher education, the failure of the government to link it to the productive process and development plans as advocated by Gandhi has led to a lopsided expansion of both general and scientific education, leading to the paradox of unemployment of the educated young in a country which urgently needs skilled manpower for its many-sided development.

There could be no worse commentary on the educational policy of the government than the migration of thousands of doctors, engineers and scientists, trained with scarce Indian resources, every year to foreign countries (thus subsidizing the economies of these countries) while the need for such skilled manpower at home in India is both great and urgent. Finally, in the absence of mass mobilization for socio-cultural change, Indian culture has remained elitist in character since independence, as it has been for thousands of years, the vast, varied and rich culture of the depressed majority including the aboriginals having failed to come to the surface and to inform the elitist culture with its vigour and vitality.

So far as social stratification is concerned, Gandhi's suggestion that class contradictions in independent India should be resolved by organized satyagraha against big landowners, capitalists and other vested interests has not been adopted by any political party or unofficial organization. The result is that class contradictions have continued to exist and even to develop in free India in spite of relatively progressive legislation by the Government, for class contradictions, as Gandhi had realized, cannot be resolved merely through legislation. As regards the caste hierarchy, Gandhi's ideas, as we have seen, were not particularly radical even in the given situation, but the basic strategy of mass mobilization for the resolution of social contradictions advocated by him could have been applied in free India to carry the process of social levelling further than Gandhi had desired. But in the absence of such mass mobilization, the radical provisions of the Indian Constitution regarding social equality have not been reflected in actual social practice; and caste, communalism, parochialism and other forces working against social equality have practically been woven into the socio-political system of independent India. Even untouchability, which is a punishable offence under the Constitution, is widely prevalent all over the country. Industrialization and higher education undoubtedly tend to undermine social prejudices to some extent; but the prospects of political and economic gain offered by them in a developing society also tend to rigidify, promote and even legitimize sectarian tendencies among a traditionally stratified people. According to some scholars, the interweaving of caste and politics has given the Indian political system an elasticity and a participatory and aggregative character which promotes democracy and equality in a real sense.[19] Although there is an element of truth in this argument, liberty and equality founded on the accommodation and aggregation of social microorganisms feeding on nothing but unreason, passion and prejudice are values of a very low quality, which one can explain but certainly not justify. Besides, the absence of mass mobilization has not only led to the injection of casteism and other prejudices into the Indian political system but also to the continuation of the traditional hegemony of the three higher castes, Brahmans, Kshatriyas and Vaishyas over the majority of the people, namely, the Shudras, the untouchables and the aboriginals (who are free from casteism).

Thus while the system and process of political change and economic development in India has been much more conducive to the ultimate values than the Chinese counterpart, the process of economic and social levelling, which is also vital to the value-oriented transformation of a traditional society, has proceeded much faster and further in China than in India, thus making the Maoist model more attractive than the Gandhian to millions of people in Asia and other parts of the world. But while the establishment of such socio-economic equality as can exist within the ambit of a fundamentally compulsive political system is the strongest point of the Maoist model of social transformation, it is certainly not a weak point of the Gandhian, for the failure to achieve socio-economic equality in India has been due, as we have seen, to the abandonment of the Gandhian technique of mass mobilization and socio-economic levelling through constructive work and satyagraha. The choice between a libertarian political system characterized by great socio-economic disparities on the one hand and a totalitarian political system characterized by a form of socio-economic equality on the other may as well be a matter of personal preference rather than of conclusive reasoning. But this surely is not a choice between the Maoist and Gandhian models, for the whole purpose of the latter is to synthesize the maximum possible socio-economic equality (though not affluence) with the maximum possible political freedom through the catalytic agent of the constructive programme and satyagraha. But even this Gandhian model, as we have seen, is not wholly conducive to the preservation and promotion of the ultimate values, in so far as it is heavily biased against rapid industrialization and technological progress. Only if a libertarian political system is combined with a nonviolent programme of mass mobilization and conflict resolution for the establishment of socio-economic equality, as advocated by Gandhi, as well as with a broad non-Gandhian programme of industrial and technological progress, shall we have the beginnings of a model of social transformation which would be truly conducive to the promotion of liberty, equality and fraternity. Without doubt, too, this would be a much more difficult model than either the Maoist or the Gandhian.

CHAPTER SIX

TOWARDS A THIRD MODEL

THE POLITICAL AND socio-cultural transformation of the Western countries in the last few centuries followed, and at least partly resulted from, the vast economic changes brought about by the Industrial Revolution and its aftermath. Rapid economic development and innovation preceded, in other words, political and social innovation and development. The process of change in contemporary Asia and Africa, on the other hand, has been a simultaneous and integral process, a process of radical political change and innovation having in fact partly preceded developments in other spheres in most cases. Secondly, while the industrialized countries of the West reached their present level of development through a process lasting several centuries since the Industrial Revolution, the Afro-Asian peoples are determined to telescope these centuries into a few decades; at any rate, they expect their governments and political leaders to make the maximum possible effort in this direction. Thirdly, on account of their historical experience of Western imperialism, and under the influence of liberal and socialist thought, partly Western and partly indigenous, leaders of public opinion in these two continents have a common measure of agreement regarding the need for avoiding the growth of a capitalist economic system. Whether it is Sun Yat-sen's China, Nehru's India, U Nu's Burma, Sukarno's Indonesia, Nasser's UAR, Nkrumah's Ghana (or other new African states), a broad and often undefined socialism has represented the consensus of the Afro-Asian intelligentsia in this century. A viable model of social transformation in this part of the globe must be squarely based on a recognition of these three basic facts.

One of the most important requisites of development in this context is the leading role of the state. The abysmal poverty, high population pressure, mass illiteracy, pluralistic and hierarchical social structure, absence of horizontal as well as vertical mobility, and the relatively rigid traditional mores of most of the Afro-Asian countries in the midst of a revolution of expectations, make it imperative for the state to act as the prime mover of change, as the entrepreneur, innovator and regulator in many diverse spheres of the development process, as Gunnar Myrdal has argued in detail.[1] Moreover, the state has to assume the role of the arbiter with regard to what Eugene Black has described as "the inevitable conflicts between growth and justice, growth and equality, growth and national power and prestige."[2] In this respect the state in the third world countries have an inevitable responsibility, the like of which was not encountered by the countries of the West in the early stages of their development, as both Myrdal and Black have pointed out. In view of the presence of traditionally strong economic and social vested interests in these societies, and the explosive demands for social and economic justice, it is also necessary to follow a rather restrictive policy with regard to private property and privilege. But the power of the state over the civil society must not be extended indefinitely so as to threaten the autonomy of the latter and of the individual seriously, since in that case the process of innovation would lead to a disvalue system. While both Mao and Gandhi are agreed on the need for state control and regulation, I have already argued that the Gandhian accent on the limitation of the power of the state is more consistent with this approach to development than the Maoist theory and practice of state.

Another major condition for the transformation of Asian and African societies in the given context is the direct participation of the masses in the resolution of social contradictions, in the reconstruction of social, political and economic institutions, and in production. The problems of these societies are so vast and complex, the obstacles to change are often so deep-rooted, the vested interests are often so well-entrenched, and the task of resource mobilization so gigantic, that the legislative and administrative processes of the state, though necessary, cannot by themselves hope to touch anything more than the fringe of the problem of change. The masses themselves must take organized and concerted direct action for resolving social contradictions, building new institutions and promoting production, if the process of development is to be reasonably rapid and meaningful. While both Mao and Gandhi are strong advocates of such direct mass action, Gandhi's constructive programme and satyagraha are more consistent with the ultimate values, as I have already argued, than Mao's mass line and people's war, although the basic Gandhian techniques must be adapted to the objective conditions of a particular developing society, with special reference to the need for rapid industrialization and technological progress.

But the problem does not end there. Mass mobilization on a big scale in a traditional society for the collective resolution of contradictions and for constructive effort seems to require something more than an awareness on the part of the masses of their enlightened self-interest. It apparently requires an emotional appeal which was provided, in the case of Gandhi's experiments in India, by the patriotism generated by foreign rule, and so far as the broad masses were concerned, by a certain quasi-religious "this-worldly asceticism" as exemplified by Gandhi, and in the case of Mao's China by ideological indoctrination, hatred of imperialism and the promise of a glorious future. Mass mobilization for resolving contradictions and for constructive work of a socio-economic nature would be much more difficult, though certainly not impossible, in an independent country with a liberal political system, where the state would be constitutionally as well as morally debarred from regimenting the population in any form, where the force of ideology would be necessarily weak, and where reason and science would replace traditional religion. The solution has to be found partly in social education—perhaps a modified and libertarian form of the systems of mass education advocated by Mao and Gandhi—and partly in the generation of local incentives through political and economic decentralization. Besides, the political rivalries of a multi-party system would tend to make unanimity of aims, objects and methods rather difficult to achieve. In order for a gigantic and voluntary mass effort to be successful, it would, therefore, be necessary to reduce political rivalry with regard to the resolution of contradictions as well as developmental work to a negligible minimum. This, in turn, would pose difficult problems of political organization which I shall discuss presently.

The central problem in the third world context is, of course, that of industrialization. Industrialization as such can take place under different and often conflicting ideologies and political systems. In England and America it has taken place under capitalism and a form of political democracy; in Germany under capitalism and an authoritarian political system which was converted into Fascism at a time of very rapid scientific, technological and industrial progress; in Japan under capitalism aided by the state; and in the Soviet Union under state ownership of means of production and a party dictatorship. But the political, economic and social disciplines required for industrialization under different political systems have been quite different. The question for the developing states of Asia and Africa is whether industrialization can be achieved at a sufficiently rapid rate so as to keep pace with the expectations of the people and the other requirements of state building including external security, without seriously compromising the basic values. The Gandhian approach to it, I have argued, does not offer the prospect of rapid industrialization, and hence fails to promote values in a true sense. The Maoist method, on the other hand, secures a rapid but unbalanced rate of industrial growth, and compromises the ultimate values rather seriously.

A major determinant of the rate of industrial growth in the early phase of industrialization is the volume of the agricultural surplus. In the Soviet-Chinese model of industrialization it is possible to raise a relatively large agricultural surplus through such institutions as the collective farms and communes, which organize production along quasi-military lines and keep agricultural consumption down to the absolute minimum. This system does not necessarily lead to a faster rate of growth of agricultural production than under other systems, as the relatively low agricultural productivity of the Soviet Union, Eastern Europe and China (compared with that of such countries as the USA and Japan) would indicate. All that the Soviet-Chinese method definitely achieves is the mobilization of a larger proportion of the agricultural production through a system of compulsory levies and state purchase of agricultural commodities at arbitrarily fixed prices. But neither the institutional regimentation of agriculture through collective farms and communes nor the mobilization of an artificially large agricultural surplus through compulsive methods would be possible in a political system where different political parties have the freedom to present alternative policies and programmes before the peasantry, and the latter has the right to express its political and economic choice through the ballot box. In such a system the main emphasis would have to be placed on increasing agricultural production through such measures as land reforms, voluntary agricultural cooperation, improved seeds, fertilizers, scientific farming, etc. The agricultural surplus would have to be mobilized through taxation and induced rural savings; and even taxation would have to be kept within narrow limits by a government which does not wish to be defeated in the next election. It is here that mass mobilization of the Gandhian type can be of considerable help, and would in fact be unavoidable if a rapid rate of industrial growth is to be achieved. But with the best of efforts a liberal political system would probably fall behind a totalitarian one-party system with regard to the volume of agricultural surplus available for industrialization.

Another crucial consideration is the priority of industrial investment. It is possible to build industrial and military power at a relatively rapid rate by investing the great bulk of the resources in heavy industry. But this strategy inevitably involves the serious and prolonged restriction of the production of consumer goods, including such basic determinants of the standard of living as food, clothing and housing. This is the pattern of industrial development followed by the Soviet Union and China, which also explains their great military power in the face of a low standard of living (the Soviet Union is much ahead of China with regard to both military power and standard of living on account of its head start and various other advantages, but the pattern is essentially the same in both the countries). This pattern of development, again, would not be possible in a political system where the people have the right to vote for a more balanced pattern which is immediately related to a rise in the standard of living. Nor would such a pattern be necessary unless it is decided to adopt an extremely militaristic view of national security and foreign policy. A liberal political system would have to strike a greater balance between heavy and consumer goods industries and, therefore, to be satisfied with less military power. As a consequence, it would have to depend at least partially on collective security as provided by the UN.

An equally important problem is the discipline of the masses of people during the period of industrialization, especially in the early phase. Such discipline consists mainly in restricting consumption and devoting full energy to productive labour. The restriction of consumption is achieved in the Soviet-Chinese model primarily through a rigorous system of state levies and rationing. While the state levies and taxes cannot be imposed beyond a certain limit under a liberal political system, rationing of essential commodities is both possible and desirable in all developing countries, since the actual beneficiaries of rationing are the majority of the people. Labour discipline is, however, a different kind of problem. In the Soviet-Chinese model a militaristic labour discipline is enforced by the state and the party alike through a rigorous system of labour laws which makes it impossible for a worker to change his place of work or occupation without the permission of the government and involves severe punishment for unpunctuality, absenteeism or negligence of duty. While some labour discipline is necessary for every industrializing country, a liberal political system with a free and competitive trade union movement cannot imitate the Soviet-Chinese pattern in this respect. In such a system a minimum necessary amount of compulsion must be supplemented by voluntarily induced discipline and hard labour. And with regard to both restriction of consumption and discipline at work, the inculcation of the virtues of frugality and hard labour through mass movements of a voluntary character would be unavoidable in a liberal political system. But in order for such mass movements to be successful it would be necessary to start such frugality and hard labour at the highest political level, as in the case of both the Gandhian and the Maoist types of leadership.

The maximum possible rate of industrialization, irrespective of the human cost involved, is not demanded even by the strongest advocates of state power. To take a rather extreme example, the pace of industrialization in populous countries like India and China can be considerably accelerated by exterminating the vast segment of population which cannot be gainfully employed in the short run and poses a difficult problem even in the long run; but no one has so far advocated such a course. Those who argue that industrialization must be consistent not merely with the preservation of human life but also with the values of liberty, equality and fraternity, go one step further and reason that the pace, direction and pattern of industrialization should be tempered by these values.

There remains the question of the nature of political organization which would be consistent with the pattern of state initiative, mass mobilization and industrialization outlined above. Practically none of the developing states of Asia and Africa have been able to establish a stable two-party system which represents the model of Western political democracy. The main reason for this is the extremely pluralistic nature of most of the developing states, which are characterized by religious, linguistic, regional, ethnic, social and cultural subdivisions to a much greater extent than the Western states. The problem of political integration caused by such pluralism is particularly acute in South and South-East Asia, although the predominance of one political party in India has imparted a measure of stability to the Indian political system which is missing from the other states in the area. This multi-dimensional pluralism of the developing societies not only makes them politically unstable, but also makes their economic and social development an extremely difficult process. In particular, the Gandhian type of mass mobilization for resolving socio-economic contradictions and for a nation-wide constructive endeavour which, as I have argued, must be an integral element of social transformation within a liberal political system, requires a broad unanimity among the people for their success, and would be impossible in a country where a multiplicity of political parties representing a whole spectrum of political opinions from the extreme left to the extreme right, or other kinds of competitive pluralistic pressure, tend to frustrate all cooperative efforts for change and development.

The political instability and relatively slow pace of socio-economic change which have resulted from this situation in many of the new states trying to develop within the framework of a liberal political system have led to various practical and theoretical consequences. The major practical consequence seems to be the emergence of military regimes tending to perpetuate themselves in many of the developing countries. The most important theoretical consequence seems to be two extreme and sharp reactions among the intelligentsia in the developing societies. One school of thought, led by followers of Gandhi like Jayaprakash Narayan (who has also borrowed heavily from the political ideas of M. N. Roy), has been advocating the establishment of a "partyless democracy" in which the existing parties would wither away under social pressure rather than be suppressed by the state. The political system would be based on direct democracy at the local level without any recognition being given to political parties, followed by indirect elections at the provincial and national levels. It would also be characterized by the maximum possible decentralization of power, with the distribution of power starting from the village and town level and proceeding upwards, the number of powers being progressively reduced at each higher level, until the central government is left with only a few but important residuary powers.

This scheme, which has largely been inspired by the anarchistic legacy of Gandhi, can hardly be regarded as an adequate answer to the problem of the political framework of development. The partyless and decentralized politics visualized in it would in all probability aggravate the centrifugal tendencies within the developing societies instead of promoting socio-political integration and economic development, and make the politics of these societies more parochial, tribalistic and communal than ever. In a system of free elections an ambitious political party is constrained to perform an aggregative function, which will probably disappear in a partyless system. Moreover, a largely depoliticized and decentralized system of this kind would be inconsistent with rapid industrialization at state initiative which, as I have argued before, is a necessary prerequisite to the value-oriented transformation of developing societies. But perhaps the greatest practical difficulty would be that of bringing such a system into existence. Since a political party provides a forum for the articulation of different interests and the aggregation of various pluralistic pressures, it is an instrument in the hands of various individuals and groups for the promotion of their material interests. The existing political parties can, therefore, be abolished not by common social pressure, but only by some form of authoritarianism which, of course, would defeat the very purpose of such a scheme.

Of greater operational significance is the other extreme reaction which is also more directly relevant to the present study. Dismayed by the political instability, relatively slow economic development, the persistence of gross socio-economic inequality, and the high incidence of military regimes among the developing nations, some sections of the intelligentsia in the new states have come to regard the Leninist-Maoist kind of party-state as the only possible vehicle for the successful transformation of the Afro-Asian states. It is such a one-party system, so the argument runs, which can truly aggregate the vast and complex centrifugal forces within the new states, plan economic development under proper central direction and control, and carry out industrialization within a short period of time. In fact, the political appeal of Maoism to otherwise non-Communist and even non-Marxist intellectuals in Asia lies mainly in the efficiency aspect of the one-party system, just as its economic appeal to them lies in telescoped industrialization. But as I have tried to show at length before, the Leninist-Maoist kind of party-state is inconsistent with a value-oriented approach to the process of political, economic and social innovation.

And yet both the anarchist and totalitarian responses represent a genuinely felt need of the traditional Afro-Asian societies trying to transform themselves, as I have already explained. The solution seems to lie in the development of a broad political platform which would aggregate a plurality of interests through an operational consensus, like the Indian National Congress, especially before independence, and the system which has come into existence in many newly independent countries of Africa under the broad ideological style of "African socialism." It is of course easier to build such a broad platform as the vehicle of a national freedom movement than as a prime mover of change after independence, when the conflict of interests becomes much more acute. But the experience of India indicates that it can be done, if the broad political platform follows a flexible and dynamic policy of ideological response and cooptation vis-à-vis the more extremist political forces which may grow up on its periphery. The fundamental freedoms including that of political organization must be constitutionally as well as operationally respected; but this should not make it impossible for a broad political platform to emerge, even where it does not exist, since the common stake in stability and development is strong enough to make this possible if the consensus method of sharing and conciliation of interests is correctly followed by one of the leading political parties, and if it dedicates itself to the task of mass mobilization for resolving socio-economic contradictions through direct and nonviolent mass action and for developmental work. At any rate, it seems clear that only such a broad and liberal political platform can transform the traditional societies in the new states of Asia and Africa at a rapid pace and consistently with the ultimate values of liberty, equality and fraternity.

Although the Maoist and Gandhian models of social transformation grew out of specific historical situations in China and India respectively, and even with regard to their broad perspectives and general characteristics are more relevant to the predominantly agricultural Asiatic and African societies than to the industrially developed countries, some of the basic ideas of Mao and Gandhi have also a bearing on the problems of industrial societies, particularly those in the process of transition to a post-industrial or technetronic age. It is with a brief comment on this subject that I shall conclude this work.

Broadly speaking, the most important problem of the industrial societies is the lag between machine technology and social technology, or to put it in another way, between technology and culture. One of the major manifestations of this lag is environmental pollution and the consequent jeopardy to society and even human life. In so far as this problem is an essential concomitant of the unrestrained growth of technology and industrialism, one section of opinion in countries like the USA has reacted by advocating a partial return to nature and the abandonment of the ethos of an affluent society in favour of that of a good society. Such other social phenomena as widespread crime, drug addiction and neurosis which are especially prevalent in Western societies (although they also seem to be growing in the Soviet Union) have strengthened this kind of reaction. It is a reaction which is very similar to Gandhi's reaction to industrialism, a problem on which Marxism and Maoism can shed no light, for they share with Western materialism the common advocacy of unrestrained material prosperity. While such reactions may be carried too far, it is obvious that the finiteness of man's material environment including the planet which he inhabits, will one day put a definite limit to the extent to which he can exploit it, and will, therefore, make the problem of further human development one of social rather than of machine technology. It is also obvious that this shift of emphasis from machine technology to social technology, though dictated primarily by the instinct of self-preservation, would involve subjective and moral problems to which the Gandhian accent on voluntary self-restraint would be singularly relevant. In fact the essence of Gandhian thinking in this respect is perhaps more relevant to societies which have already reached a high level of industrialization and material affluence, than to the economically backward societies where a policy of restraining industrial and technological growth would have, as I have argued before, a disvalue effect.

Another manifestation of the lag between technology and culture in the highly industrialized societies is the inability to resolve social contradictions in the midst of superior technical know-how, material affluence and growth of knowledge in general. One such contradiction is that between the blacks and the whites in the USA. This is a problem to which the ideas of both Mao and Gandhi are obviously relevant, and both of them have found followers among the American blacks. Mao repeatedly urged the negroes of the USA to rise in arms against the government and strongly criticized the methods advocated by Martin Luther King, on the ground that the problem of race is essentially one of class antagonism which cannot be resolved except through armed struggle. He has apparently been able to influence a small section of black Americans by the idea of the revolution and of "power to the people." A more powerful though temporary impact was, however, made by Dr King and his nonviolent movement which admittedly drew its inspiration from Gandhi. With regard to certain other contradictions of industrial societies as well, for example, the contradiction between the "corporate" state and the "atomized" individual, both Mao and Gandhi seem to have found large numbers of followers generally among the younger generation, especially within the New Left all over the Western world, although many of these followers probably have rather misconceived and romanticized notions regarding the ideas of the masters.

I have already argued in detail in favour of the Gandhian method of resolving social contradictions as opposed to the Maoist method, and will not repeat the arguments here. I would only add that both from the positive and negative points of view, a technologically advanced and affluent society provides greater scope for the success-ful application of nonviolence in social relations than a technological-ly backward and poor society. The first positive factor in the situa-tion is that material affluence eliminates the economic desperation which in the poor countries tends to promote violence. It is probably much easier for people whose basic requirements of life have been satisfied and who have experienced a measure of material well-being to get used to a nonviolent mode of conduct than for people whose lives are still primarily a struggle for the material necessities of life. Secondly, the growth of human knowledge which accompanies scientific and technological advance should help to create an enlight-ened self-interest among people in the industrial societies, whereas the absence of such knowledge in the pre-industrial societies is likely to result in the manifestation of untamed instincts and passions. The negative factor in the social milieu of the industrial societies which facilitates the growth of nonviolence is that violence combined with high technology would cause unacceptable damage to society, and the instinct of self-preservation should dictate a policy of nonviolence in a high-technology society.

Obviously, too, the forms of nonviolent action in the industrial and post-industrial societies will have to vary considerably from those innovated by Gandhi in a given socio-historical context, for while truth is inherent in the generalized essence of nonviolent action, it is not inseparable from the particular form such action may take in a given historical situation. In fact, only a new form of nonviolent action for the resolution of social contradictions, innovated by a new leader or group of leaders, can hope to succeed in the unique situation of the industrial and technetronic societies. As Erik H. Erikson has observed: "Gandhi's instrument, once innovated by one of the rarest of men under specific cultural and historical conditions, now exists in the images, impulses, and ritualizations of many who have become aware of it by what we may call 'ritual diffusion'. It now calls for leaders who will re-innovate it elsewhere, sharing, no doubt, some of the personal and historical motivation of the first leader, the first followers, and those first led, but recombining this motivation with totally new elements. For if the instrument was once 'the truth', it can and must become actual in entirely different settings, in which the necessary tool-making may be used on a different and yet analogous tradition, and where the toolmakers come from different vocations and yet share converging goals. If truth is actuality, it can never consist of mere repetition of ritualized acts or stances. It calls for reconstitution by a new combination of universal verities and social disciplines."[3]

With regard to external contradictions among nations, too, Gandhi's ideas are becoming increasingly more meaningful than the nuclear stance adopted by the USA, the Soviet Union and Mao's China, in the context of the vast nuclear annihilation staring humanity in the face. The influence of nonviolent thinking with regard to international relations is already apparent in the spectacular growth of the pacifist movement, especially among the younger generation, all over the Western world, and even in the Soviet Union where it has been voiced in *samizdat* literature, in the writings of such literary stalwarts as Pasternak and Solzhenitsyn and such scientific geniuses as Sakharov. The application of nonviolence in international relations will doubtless be infinitely more difficult than its application in domestic affairs, and will probably have to be induced by many more shocks and disasters as well as the centralization of nuclear power in a world organization vastly more powerful than the UN. But the overkill potential of nuclear weapons has left humanity with no other rational choice.

Gandhi presented a limited concept of man when he generally went against science and technology and overemphasized man's metaphysical nature. But perhaps, after science and technology have satisfied man's material needs, the Gandhian emphasis on the metaphysical nature of man would prove to be singularly relevant to the problem of relations among men and nations in the nuclear and technetronic age. For high technology geared to violence—the common characteristic of Western and Communist states—will almost inevitably destroy the human race with all its achievements and aspirations; while, combined with nonviolence, it may yet bring us close to some of the utopias, including the Maoist and the Gandhian, which rare and visionary human beings have dreamt of from time immemorial.

NOTES

CHAPTER ONE

1. In view of the ambiguity and confusion surrounding the term "moderniza-tion," and its doubtful applicability to the present study as explained at the end of Chapter II, I have avoided the use of this term in this book, and used instead such terms as "transformation," "change," "development," etc.

2. For a detailed study of nationalism and Communism in China see Chalmers Johnson: *Peasant Nationalism and Communist Power*, Stanford University Press, Stanford, 1962; for the Sinification of Marxism-Leninism by Mao see Stuart Schram: *The Political Thought of Mao Tse-tung*, Pelican, 1969, Chs. I, II. For a historical survey of the nationalist basis of the Indian freedom movement see R. C. Majumdar: *History of the Freedom Movement in India*, 3 vols, Firma K. L. Mukhopadhyay, Calcutta, 1963.

3. Bertrand Russell: *The Problem of China*, George Allen & Unwin, London, 1922, pp. 242-45.

4. Harold Isaacs: *The Tragedy of the Chinese Revolution*, Stanford University Press, Stanford, 1962, pp. 53-56.

5. J. Bandyopadhyaya: *Indian Nationalism Versus International Communism: The Role of Ideology in International Politics*, Firma K. L. Mukhopadhyay, Calcutta, 1966.

6. For a comparison of land yields in pre-revolutionary China and pre-indepen-dence India see J. L. Buck: *Land Utilization in China*, University of Nanking, 1939, reproduced by the Council of Economic and Cultural Affairs, New York, 1956, pp. 224-25. For food production trends in pre-revolutionary China see J. L. Buck: "Foodgrains Production in Mainland China Before and During the Communist Regime," in Buck, Wu and Dawson: *Food and Agriculture in Communist China*, Praeger, New York, 1966. For the applica-tion of fertilizers in pre-revolutionary Chinese agriculture see D. A. Perkins: *Agricultural Development in China, 1368-1968*, Aldine, Chicago, 1969, pp. 27, 37ff. For agricultural production trends, soil fertility and application of fertilizers in British India see G. Blyn: *Agricultural Trends in India, 1891-1947: Output, Availability and Productivity*, University of Pennsylvania Press, 1966.

7. Barrington Moore: *Social Origins of Dictatorship and Democracy*, Beacon Press, Boston, 1967, Ch. IV.

8. Mao Tse-tung: *Selected Works*, vol. II, Foreign Languages Press, Peking, 1965, pp. 305-34. Hereinafter referred to as *Selected Works*.

9. See L. Natarajan: *Peasant Uprisings in India, 1849-1900*, Bombay, 1953.

10. See A. L. Basham: *The Wonder that was India*, Sidgwick & Jackson, London, 1954, pp. 66, 213, 282.

11. G. W. F. Hegel: *Reason in History—A General Introduction to the Philosophy of History*, tr. Robert S. Hartman, Bobbs-Merrill Co., New York, 1953, pp. 76-77; Karl Marx: "British Rule in India," *New York Daily Tribune*, June 25, 1853, incorporated in *On Colonialism*, Foreign Languages Publishing House, Moscow, undated [1960?]; Max Weber: *The Religion of India*, Free Press, New York, 1968, pp. 144-47, 333-38; *The Protestant Ethic and the Rise of Capitalism*, Charles Scribner's Sons, New York, 1958, pp. 19-25.

12. See Franz Schurmann: *Ideology and Organization in Communist China*, California University Press, Berkeley, 1970, Ch. VII.

13. Karl Marx: *op. cit.*

14. For the best available study of the early influences on Mao see Stuart Schram: *Mao Tse-tung*, Pelican, 1966, Chs. I-III. For Mao's own account of his formative years see Edgar Snow: *Red Star Over China*, Grove Press, New York, 1961, Part IV.

15. Stuart Schram: *Mao Tse-tung*, p. 25.

16. Stuart Schram: *The Political Thought of Mao Tse-tung*, p. 22.

17. Edgar Snow: *op. cit.*, p. 155.

18. For the formative influences on Gandhi see M. K. Gandhi: *An Autobiography or the Story of My Experiments with Truth*, Navajivan Publishing House, Ahmedabad, 1958; Erik H. Erikson: *Gandhi's Truth*, W. W. Norton & Co., New York, 1969, Part II; B. R. Nanda: *Mahatma Gandhi—A Biography*, George Allen & Unwin, London, 1959, Chs. I, II.

CHAPTER TWO

1. Mao Tse-tung: *Selected Military Writings*, Foreign Languages Press, Peking, 1963, p. 227. Hereinafter referred to as *Selected Military Writings*.

2. *Selected Works*, vol. IV, p. 414.

3. For a detailed study of the ultimate values in Gandhian thought see J. Bandyopadhyaya: *Social and Political Thought of Gandhi*, Allied Publishers, Calcutta, 1969, Part I.

4. *Ibid.*, Ch. VI.

5. *Harijan*, July 28, 1946.

6. M. K. Gandhi: *Economic and Industrial Life and Relations*, 3 vols, Navajivan Publishing House, Ahmedabad, 1959; J. Bandyopadhyaya: *Social and Political Thought of Gandhi*, Ch. VIII.

7. D. G. Tendulkar: *Mahatma—Life of Mohandas Karamchand Gandhi*, Publications Division, Government of India, Delhi, 1960, vol. II, p. 161. This is an 8-volume biography of Gandhi compiled by his secretary, which was corrected and authorized by him before publication and is generally regarded as a standard primary source on the life and thought of Gandhi. Hereinafter referred to as *Mahatma*.

8. *Ibid.*, vol. IV, p. 11.

9. *Harijan*, June 22, 1935.

10. *Harijan*, April 20, 1940.

11. *Mahatma*, vol. VII, p. 188.
12. *Ibid.*, p. 223.
13. *Ibid.*, p. 334.
14. *Harijan*, March 9, 1947.
15. S. N. Agarwal: *The Gandhian Plan of Economic Development for India*, Padma Publications, Bombay, 1944.
16. Karl Marx and Frederick Engels: *Selected Works*, Progress Publishers, Moscow, 1968, p. 430.
17. *Young India*, September 3, 1925.
18. *On Khrushchev's Phoney Communism and its Historical Lessons for the World*, Foreign Languages Press, Peking, 1964, pp. 5, 8, 13, 15, 33-59, 65, 70-71. It was first published as a joint editorial in *Renmin Ribao* and *Hung Ch'i* in July 1964 in reply to Khrushchev's speech at the 22nd Congress of the CPSU.
19. Quoted in Stuart Schram: *The Political Thought of Mao Tse-tung*, pp. 303-4.
20. F. Engels: *Anti-Dühring*, Foreign Languages Publishing House, Moscow, 1959, p. 477.
21. *Selected Works*, vol. I, p. 339.
22. Tagore's views were expressed in three letters published in *Modern Review*, May 1921 and an article entitled "The Call of Truth" in *Modern Review*, October 1951. Gandhi's reply took the form of two articles in *Young India*, dated June 1 and October 31, 1921.
23. M. K. Gandhi: *Constructive Programme*, Navajivan Publishing House, Ahmedabad, 1948, pp. 20-21.
24. *Young India*, May 10, 1928, December 5, 1929; *Harijan*, June 9, 1946.
25. *Selected Works*, vol. I, pp. 321-22.
26. *Selected Works*, vol. I, pp. 326-28, vol. II, pp. 503 ff., vol. III, pp. 255 ff.
27. Mao Tse-tung: *On the Correct Handling of Contradictions Among the People*, Foreign Languages Press, Peking, 1966, p. 19. Hereinafter referred to as *On the Correct Handling of Contradictions*.
28. See Stuart Schram: *The Political Thought of Mao Tse-tung*, pp. 296-98.
29. *Selected Works*, vol. II, pp. 224-25.
30. *Ibid.*, p. 220.
31. *Ibid.*, pp. 219-20.
32. *Ibid.*, pp. 220-21.
33. *Selected Works*, vol. I, p. 322.
34. *Mahatma*, vol. II, p. 255.
35. *Collected Works of Mahatma Gandhi*, vol. X, Publications Division, Government of India, 1963, p. 43.
36. *Young India*, July 17, 1924.
37. *Young India*, December 26, 1924.
38. *Harijan*, May 27, 1939.
39. *Mahatma*, vol. III, p. 216.
40. See J. Bandyopadhyaya: *Social and Political Thought of Gandhi*, Ch. 2.
41. N. K. Bose: *Selections From Gandhi*, Navajivan Publishing House, Ahmedabad, 1947, p. 93.
42. *Mahatma*, vol. II, pp. 2-12.
43. *Young India*, May 1, 1920.

44. M. K. Gandhi: *Communism and Communists*, Navajivan Publishing House, Ahmedabad, 1959, p. 4.
45. *Mahatma*, vol. II, p. 333.
46. *Ibid.*, vol. III, p. 135.
47. *Ibid.*, vol. V, p. 9.
48. *Ibid.*, vol. II, p. 333.
49. M. K. Gandhi: *Communism and Communists*, p. 6.
50. *Ibid.*
51. *Mahatma*, vol. VI, p. 38.
52. *Ibid.*, vol. IV, p. 194.
53. *Ibid.*, vol. VI, p. 97.
54. *Ibid.*
55. *Ibid.*, vol. IV, p. 280.
56. *Ibid.*, p. 312.
57. *Young India*, October 7, 1926.
58. See J. Bandyopadhyaya: *Social and Political Thought of Gandhi*, pp. 146-47.
59. M. K. Gandhi: *Communism and Communists*, p. 17.
60. *Mahatma*, vol. V, p. 277.
61. *Ibid.*, p. 339.
62. *Ibid.*, vol. VI, p. 103.
63. *Ibid.*, p. 266.
64. *Ibid.*, vol. V, p. 336.
65. *Quotations From Chairman Mao Tse-tung*, Foreign Languages Press, Peking, second edition, 1967, p. iii.
66. Edgar Snow: "Interview with Mao," *The New Republic*, February 27, 1965, p. 23.
67. See Joan Robinson: *The Cultural Revolution*, Pelican, 1968.
68. Stuart Schram: *op. cit.*, p. 79.
69. Franz Schurmann: *op. cit.*, pp. 513, 525.
70. M. K. Gandhi: *Hindu Dharma*, Navajivan Publishing House, Ahmedabad, 1950, p. 69.
71. N. K. Bose: *Studies in Gandhism*, Calcutta, 1962, p. 15.
72. See N. K. Bose: *Selections From Gandhi*, pp. 48-52; *Young India*, September 20, 1928; *Harijan*, February 23, 1947.

CHAPTER THREE

1. *Selected Military Writings*, pp. 227, 228.
2. *Ibid.*, p. 228.
3. *Ibid.*, p. 217.
4. Lin Piao: "Long Live the Victory of the People's War," *Peking Review*, September 3, 1965, p. 19.
5. *Ibid.*, p. 14.
6. See Mao Tse-tung: "Strategy in China's Revolutionary War," *Selected Military Writings*, pp. 75-150.

7. Barrington Moore: *op. cit.*, p. 192; Paul M. Lindebarger: *The China of Chiang Kaishek*, Boston, 1941, pp. 147-48.

8. *Young India*, February 27, 1930.

9. See Joan V. Bondurant: *The Conquest of Violence*, University of California Press, Berkeley, 1965, p. 104.

10. *Selected Military Writings*, pp. 9 ff., 75 ff., 151 ff., 313 ff. See also Lin Piao: *op. cit.*, pp. 16, 18, 19.

11. See Stuart Schram: *The Political Thought of Mao Tse-tung*, p. 407; "Spring Thunder Over India" and "Raising the Red Flag in India," *Peking Review*, July 24, 1967; "The Indian Food Crisis and Armed Revolution," *Peking Review*, September 22, 1967.

12. Lin Piao: *op. cit.*, p. 24.

13. *Renmin Ribao* editorial on "People's War is Invincible," reproduced in *Peking Review*, July 24, 1967, pp. 8-10.

14. Mao Tse-tung: *People of the World Unite and Defeat the US Aggressors and Their Running Dogs* (statement of May 20, 1970), Foreign Languages Press, Peking, 1970, pp. 3-7.

15. See *Mahatma*, vol. IV, pp. 312 ff., vol. V, pp. 17-18.

16. See *Mahatma*, vol. IV, pp. 319-21, vol. V, p. 160, vol. VI, pp. 135, 295-96; *Harijan*, October 8, 1938, June 18, 1940, July 3, 1940, March 16, 1942.

17. *Harijan*, November 4, 1939, June 17, 1940.

18. *Selected Works*, vol. IV, p. 100.

19. Lin Piao: *op. cit.*, p. 26.

20. *Ibid.*, p. 27.

21. See Stuart Schram: *The Political Thought of Mao Tse-tung*, p. 409. Later Chinese and Soviet accounts disclosed that the foreign statesman referred to by Mao was the Indian Prime Minister, Jawaharlal Nehru.

22. Lin Piao: *op. cit.*, p. 28.

23. For a discussion of the official Chinese view of China's nuclear weapons programme see symposium on "China and the Bomb" by Morton H. Halperin, William R. Harris and Hungdah Chin, *China Quarterly*, January-March, No. 21, 1965. See also Ralph L. Powell: "Great Powers and Atomic Bombs are Paper Tigers," *China Quarterly*, July-September, No. 23, 1965.

24. Lin Piao: *op. cit.*, p. 29.

25. Jhaveri and Tendulkar: *Mahatma*, Bombay, vol. VII, 1953, p. 31.

26. *Ibid.*, pp. 46, 84.

27. *Ibid.*, pp. 60-61.

28. *Ibid.*, p. 101.

29. *Ibid.*, pp. 171-72.

30. *Ibid.*, p. 248.

31. See Edgar Snow: "Interview with Mao," *The New Republic*, February 27, 1965, p. 18.

32. See N. K. Bose: *Selections From Gandhi*, pp. 72, 90, 154.

33. Lin Piao: *op. cit.*, p. 18.

34. *Selected Military Writings*, p. 70.

35. Lin Piao: *op. cit.*, p. 18.

36. *Selected Military Writings*, p. 347.

37. Lin Piao: *op. cit.*, p. 18.

38. See Mao Tse-tung: "Problems of Strategy in China's Revolutionary War," "Problems of Strategy in Guerilla War Against Japan," "On Protracted War" and "Problems of War and Strategy" in *Selected Military Writings.*

39. For an analysis of the detailed tactics employed in five major satyagrahas in India, see Joan V. Bondurant: *op. cit.*, Ch. III.

40. *Young India*, July 28, 1920; *Mahatma*, vol. I, p. 300.

41. *Young India*, September 22, 1920.

42. *Mahatma*, vol. II, p. 21.

43. *Young India*, March 27, 1930.

44. *Mahatma*, vol. V, pp. 294, 390.

45. See K. Shridharani: *War Without Violence*, Bharatiya Vidya Bhavan, Bombay, 1962, pp. 49-50; *Harijan*, June 17, 1940, June 22, 1940.

46. *Harijan*, March 16, 1942.

47. Quoted, K. Shridharani: *op. cit.*, p. 49.

48. *Harijan*, November 4, 1939.

49. Quoted, K. Shridharani: *op. cit.*, pp. 49-50.

50. *Young India*, December 5, 1929; *Harijan*, March 31, 1946.

51. Erik H. Erikson: *op. cit.* This strike is in fact the nucleus round which the whole fabric of Erikson's study of Gandhi is built.

52. *Harijan*, March 31, 1946.

53. M. K. Gandhi: *India's Case for Swaraj*, ed. W. P. Kabadi, Bombay, 1932, p. 394.

54. For a collection of Gandhi's writings on industrial relations and strikes see M. K. Gandhi: *Economic and Industrial Life and Relations*, 3 vols, Navajivan Publishing House, Ahmedabad, 1959.

55. Erik H. Erikson: *op. cit.*, p. 448.

56. *Ibid.*, p. 399.

57. See Jacques Maritain: *Man and the State*, University of Chicago Press, Chicago, 1961, p. 69; Karl Jaspers: *The Future of Mankind*, tr. E. B. Ashton, University of Chicago Press, Chicago, 1961, pp. 39-40; W. K. Hancock: *Four Studies of War and Peace in this Country*, Cambridge University Press, Cambridge, 1961, pp. 81-84; J. Bandyopadhyaya: *Social and Political Thought of Gandhi*, Ch. XVI.

58. For an analysis of the major historical experiments with nonviolent resistance against foreign occupation, see Mulford Q. Sibley: *The Quiet Battle*, Bharatiya Vidya Bhavan, Bombay 1965; Ted Dunn: *Alternatives to War and Violence*, James Clarke & Co., London, 1963.

59. See Bertrand Russell: *Justice in Wartime*, Allen & Unwin, London, 1924; *Commonsense and Nuclear Warfare*, Allen & Unwin, London, 1961; Sir Stephen King-Hall: *Defence in the Nuclear Age*, Victor Gollancz, London, 1958; B. H. Liddell Hart: *Deterrent or Defence*, Stevens & Sons, London, 1960, Ch. 20.

60. For an analysis of the success or failure of the major satyagraha campaigns led or inspired by Gandhi in South Africa and India, see J. Bandyopadhyaya: *Social and Political Thought of Gandhi*, Chs. XIII-XV; Joan V. Bondurant: *op. cit.*, Ch. III; K. Shridharani: *op. cit.*

61. Jawaharlal Nehru: *An Autobiography*, Bodley Head, London, 1947, p. 76.
62. Quoted, Michael Brecher: *Nehru: A Political Biography*, Oxford University Press, London, 1959, p. 79.
63. Erik H. Erikson: *op. cit.*, p. 391.
64. *Ibid.*, pp. 401, 423-36.

CHAPTER FOUR

1. *Selected Works*, vol. III, p. 119.
2. Mao Tse-tung: *The Socialist Upsurge in China's Countryside*, Foreign Languages Press, Peking, 1957, p. 14.
3. *Selected Works*, vol. I, p. 150.
4. See M. K. Gandhi: *Constructive Programme*, pp. 21-22, 28-29.
5. *Ibid.*, pp. 5-7.
6. *Harijan*, June 10, 1939.
7. See J. Bandyopadhyaya: *Social and Political Thought of Gandhi*, p. 155.
8. See Gunnar Myrdal: *Asian Drama*, Pantheon, New York, 1968, vol. II, Part V.
9. *Selected Works*, vol. IV, pp. 235-36.
10. See Mao Tse-tung: *The Question of Agricultural Cooperation*, Foreign Languages Press, Peking, 1956.
11. *Renmin Ribao*, May 3, 1958, quoted, Cheng Chu-yuan: *People's Communes*, V.R.I. Press, Hong Kong, 1959, p. 7.
12. *Renmin Ribao*, September 30, 1958, quoted, *ibid*, p. 109.
13. *Renmin Ribao*, October 3, 1958, quoted, *ibid.*, p. 110.
14. Ch'en Yu: "Raise High the Red Flag of the General Line, Fight to Win New Great Victories," *Nan-fang Ribao*, October 12, 1959, quoted, *Survey of China Mainland Press*, Hong Kong, No. 2191, February 8, 1960, p. 37.
15. See Jones and Poleman: "Communes and the Agricultural Crisis in China," *Food Research Institute Studies*, Stanford University, vol. III, No. 1, February 1962, p. 9.
16. See J. Bandyopadhyaya: *Social and Political Thought of Gandhi*, p. 155.
17. M. K. Gandhi: *Constructive Programme*, p. 12.
18. *Harijan*, January 27, 1940.
19. For a discussion of the educational system of the People's Republic of China see C. T. Hu: "Communist Education: Theory and Practice," and Immanuel C. Y. Hsu: "The Reorganization of Higher Education in Communist China" in Roderick MacFarquhar: *China Under Mao*, the MIT Press, 1966; Leo A. Orleans: "Communist China's Education: Policies, Problems and Prospects," in *An Economic Profile of Mainland China*, vol. 2, Studies prepared for the Joint Economic Committee, Congress of the United States, Washington, 1967; J. C. Cheng: "The Educational System in Modern and Contemporary China," in E. Stuart Kirby (ed.): *Contemporary China*, Hong Kong University Press, 1960; Marianne Bastid: " Economic Necessity and Political Ideals in Educational Reform During the Cultural Revolution," *China Quarterly*, No. 42, April-June 1970.

20. For a compilation of Gandhi's writings on education, see M. K. Gandhi: *Basic Education*, 1951; *True Education*, 1962; and *Toward New Education*, 1963—all published by Navajivan Publishing House, Ahmedabad.
21. *Harijan*, October 9, 1937.
22. *On the Correct Handling of Contradictions*, pp. 51-52.
23. See Stuart Schram: *The Political Thought of Mao Tse-tung*, p. 351.
24. *Young India*, December 29, 1920.
25. N. K. Bose: *Selections From Gandhi*, p. 264.
26. *Young India*, November 24, 1927. See also *Harijan*, September 28, 1934.
27. *Young India*, October 6, 1921.
28. *Harijan*, March 6, 1937.
29. *Harijan*, February 11, 1933.
30. See *Mahatma*, vol. VIII, p. 220.
31. *Ibid.*, vol. VIII, p. 256.
32. See M. K. Gandhi: *All Religions Are True*, Bharatiya Vidya Bhavan, Bombay, 1962; *The Way to Communal Harmony*, Navajivan Publishing House, Ahmedabad, 1963.
33. *Selected Works*, vol. II, p. 331.
34. *Ibid.*, vol. III, p. 318.
35. *Quotations From Chairman Mao Tse-tung*, p. 2.
36. *On the Correct Handling of Contradictions*, p. 3.
37. *Selected Works*, vol. II, p. 224.
38. *Ibid.*, vol. I, p. 106.
39. See Mao Tse-tung: "Pay Attention to Economic Work," *Selected Works*, vol. I; "Production is Also Possible in the Guerilla Zones" and "On Production by the Army for its Own Support and on the Importance of the Great Movements for Rectification and for Production," *Selected Works*, vol. III; and "Turn the Army into a Production Force," *Selected Works*, vol. IV.
40. See "Make Our Army a Great School of Mao Tse-tung's Thought," editorial in *Liberation Army Daily*, August 1, 1968, reproduced in *Peking Review*, August 5, 1968.
41. *Renmin Ribao*, September 4, 1958, quoted, Cheng Chu-yuan: *op. cit.*, pp. 27-28.
42. *Peking Review*, March 15, 1968, p. 5.
43. This was reported on live television in the USA from Peking by American journalists who accompanied President Nixon to Peking in February 1972 and were taken on a conducted tour of the Peking University.
44. Quoted, R. P. Stuttmier: "Party Views on Science: The Record from the First Decade," *China Quarterly*, No. 44, October-December 1970.
45. See Stuart Schram: *The Political Thought of Mao Tse-tung*, p. 323.
46. In August 1958, for example, Mao said: "It is better to set up people's communes. Their advantage lies in the fact that they combine industry, agriculture, commerce, education and military affairs. This is convenient for leadership." See Stuart Schram: *The Political Thought of Mao Tse-tung*, p. 350.
47. *Harijan*, December 30, 1939.
48. *Mahatma*, vol. VI, p. 152.
49. *Ibid.*, vol. VII, pp. 331-32.

50. *Ibid.*, vol. VIII, p. 229.
51. *Ibid.*, p. 234.
52. *Ibid.*, p. 283.
53. *Ibid.*, p. 284.
54. *Ibid.*, vol. V, p. 283.

CHAPTER FIVE

1. Speech delivered at the First Plenary Session of the Chinese People's Political Consultative Conference, September 21, 1949; quoted, Stuart Schram: *The Political Thought of Mao Tse-tung*, pp. 167-68.
2. *Selected Works*, vol. I, p. 29.
3. *On the Correct Handling of Contradictions*, p. 27.
4. Radio Moscow, April 7, 1969.
5. *New York Times*, editorial, June 2, 1959.
6. See Richard Walker: *The Human Cost of Communism in China*, prepared for the use of the Committee on the Judiciary, US Senate, US Government Printing Office, Washington, 1971, pp. 8-16.
7. See Karl A. Wittfogel: "Forced Labour in Communist China," *Problems of Communism*, July-August, 1956.
8. UNESCO: *Forced Labour*, Document E/2815, December 15, 1955, pp. 92 ff.
9. Radio Moscow, May 30, 1967.
10. *On Khrushchev's Phoney Communism and Its Historical Lessons for the World*, Foreign Languages Press, Peking, 1964, pp. 30-31.
11. See J. Bandyopadhyaya: *The Making of India's Foreign Policy*, Allied Publishers, Calcutta, 1970, Chs. III, V; Erich Schrader: "Mahatma Gandhi and the Formulation of the Foreign Policy Principles of India," *United Asia*, November-December, 1968.
12. See Nai-Ruenn Chen and Walter Galenson: *The Chinese Economy Under Communism*, Aldine, Chicago, 1969, Ch. 9; Robert M. Field: "Chinese Communist Industrial Production," *An Economic Profile of Mainland China*, vol. I, pp. 271-95; P. Bardhan: "Agriculture in China and India: output, input and prices," *Economic and Political Weekly*, Annual Number, Bombay, January 1969.
13. Government of India: *Fourth Five-Year Plan, 1969-74*, Delhi, undated [1970], Ch. 17.
14. Bertrand Russell: "In Search of Peace," in Rafiq Zakaria (ed.): *A Study of Nehru*, Jaico Publishing House, Bombay, 1964, p. 220.
15. For a compilation of Gandhi's writings on rural self-government see M. K. Gandhi: *Village Swaraj*, Navajivan Publishing House, Ahmedabad, 1963.
16. See George Rosen: *Democracy and Economic Change in India*, University of California Press, 1967, pp. 92-101.
17. Gunnar Myrdal: *op. cit.*, vol. II, Ch. 25.
18. Government of India: *Fourth Five-Year Plan*, p. 229.

19. See Lloyd I. Rudolph and Susanne H. Rudolph: *The Modernity of Tradition —Political Development in India,* University of Chicago Press, 1967, Part I.

CHAPTER SIX

1. Gunnar Myrdal: *op. cit.,* vol. II, pp. 715-20.
2. Eugene Black: *The Diplomacy of Economic Development,* Cambridge, Mass. 1961, p. 13.
3. Erik H. Erikson: *op. cit.,* pp. 435-36.

INDEX